HI, I'M AN ATHEIST!

HI, I'M AN ATHEIST!

What That Means and How to Talk About It with Others

DAVID G. McAFEE

ST. MARTIN'S
ESSENTIALS
NEW YORK

Published in the United States by St. Martin's Essentials,
an imprint of St. Martin's Publishing Group

www.stmartins.com

Designed by Steven Seighman

Library of Congress Cataloging-in-Publication Data

Names: McAfee, David G., author.
Title: Hi, I'm an atheist! : what that means and how to talk
    about it with others / David G. McAfee.
Description: First St. Martin's essentials edition. | New York :
    St. Martin's Essentials, [2021] | Includes index.
Identifiers: LCCN 2021021937 | ISBN 9781250782083
    (trade paperback) | ISBN 9781250782090 (ebook)
Subjects: LCSH: Atheism. | Atheism—Apologetic works.
Classification: LCC BL2747.3 .M3528 2021 |
    DDC 211/.8—dc23
LC record available at https://lccn.loc.gov/2021021937

Our books may be purchased in bulk for promotional,
educational, or business use. Please contact your local
bookseller or the Macmillan Corporate and Premium Sales
Department at 1-800-221-7945, extension 5442, or by email at
MacmillanSpecialMarkets@macmillan.com.

Originally published in the United States by
Dangerous Little Books in 2012.
Also published in the United States by
Hypatia Press in 2019.

First St. Martin's Essentials Edition: 2021

10 9 8 7 6 5 4 3 2 1

To my mom and dad, who never let differences of opinion stand in the way of treating me with love and respect, and to my lovely wife, Rae

CONTENTS

CONTENTS

PREFACE

"Hi, I'm an atheist." It's amazing how much those few words can accomplish at times, especially considering that one sentence doesn't really tell you much about me. It tells you I don't believe in any deities. It tells you I'm probably not part of an organized religion. But it doesn't tell you anything about my goals, what I value, or the moral philosophies on which I base my life. It doesn't let you know where my passions lie, nor does it reveal that the smell of lemons always brings a smile to my face, in part because it reminds me of the farm my grandparents had when I was growing up.

In the grand scheme of things, my simple identification as a nonbeliever in god(s) gives you almost no helpful information about who I really am as a person. Yet hearing that simple sentence—"I'm an atheist"—can be perceived as confrontational by some people. It can also cause certain believers to assume the worst of someone, spawning thoughts of devil worshippers conjuring ancient spirits in velvet robes at night. In some regions of the world, that statement can also result in threats, discrimination, and even physical violence from believers. Even as I write this in the 2020s, there are a few nations where being open about one's lack of faith can result in government-ordered execution.

Contrary to the stigma against atheism in many places throughout the world, there's nothing wrong with being an atheist or talking openly about it. And there's nothing about saying, "I'm an atheist," that is inherently hateful, condescending, or in your face. It's the same as saying, "I'm unconvinced." So, what does it actually mean to be an atheist? It simply means that you don't believe in any divine figures. So, the devil worshipper from the scenario described above couldn't be an atheist, by definition. The devil is just another side of the god coin.

The "atheist" label doesn't even describe the certainty with which you hold your beliefs, or lack thereof. Just as is the case with believers, one individual might be completely certain while another may have numerous serious doubts. An atheist or a theist would be equally capable of being agnostic in terms of their knowledge while still expressing their personal beliefs.

You probably know lots of atheists, even if you don't know it. They can be any age or gender and have any political orientation in the world. According to the latest data, 3.1 percent of people in the United States are atheists who openly refer to themselves as such. Considering that research led by a Columbia professor has shown that the average American knows about 600 people, we can safely say that the typical person in the United States knows about 18.6 avowed nonbelievers. That's pretty surprising, right? And it kind of makes you wonder about that 0.6 of a person.

Well, what if I told you that number might be even higher than people think? To understand why, we first must learn about the stigma associated with the word *atheism* itself. For starters, Americans admit to feeling cold toward atheists, a designation that is less trusted than just about every faith out there, according to the Pew Research Center. But even beyond that, the United States has a vast Christian population and even Christian-influenced culture. As such, there's an unbelievable amount of misinformation out there, often beginning with fire-and-brimstone preachers spreading it to their unsuspecting flock, about atheists and what we actually believe. Although Christianity is most popular, atheists coming from non-Christian religious groups, such as Judaism, Islam, Hinduism, and even theistic Buddhism, can also be the victims of religious misinformation like this.

When some people hear the word *atheist,* they don't think about someone who lacks belief in deities. Instead, because of the negative connotations, a lot of people think about demons or Satan worshippers, or maybe just an arrogant know-it-all who claims that there are no gods. Either way, these stereotypes are in some cases exaggerations and in others impossible. We can't control what people think of or associate with atheism, but we can do our best to reshape the narrative and spread facts, all while encouraging atheists to be themselves.

That's what I hope to do with this book.

AUTHOR'S NOTE: BORN ATHEIST

It is an interesting and demonstrable fact, that all children are atheists and were religion not inculcated into their minds, they would remain so.

—ERNESTINE LOUISE ROSE, SUFFRAGIST, ABOLITIONIST, AND FREETHINKER

To properly understand this guide to talking openly to others about atheism, some might wish to learn more about the particular context in which I, as a secular author, am writing.

The way I see it, everybody is born an atheist, and without submersion into religion as a child, we would most likely maintain that position. More often than not, however, this is not the case. In most instances, a child is taught early on that their parents' religion is the truth—and all others are evil. This mindset is rarely shaken, and those beliefs are often passed to further generations. Luckily, for me, that didn't happen.

I don't remember a particular time in my life in which I believed in the validity of a particular religious tradition. But, eventually, even I had to break the news to my family and become open regarding my secular mindset. That is because I lived in the United States, where theism is the assumed position.

My parents were not always religious people; they may have abused substances religiously—but when I was very young, church was probably the last thing on their minds. When I was two years old, my parents divorced and began their separate lives pursuing drugs to feed their addictions; thankfully, my grandmother volunteered to care for me until my mother or father could afford (financially and emotionally) to raise me. She never mistreated me or abused me, but she was the first person in my life to introduce me to religion and the authority of the Christian church. My grandparents with whom I spent the majority of my early childhood considered themselves Fundamentalist Baptist Christians—and I was raised in a way that, they thought, would encourage similar ideologies in me.

When I was a bit older—around six years old—I went to a Christian church with my grandparents; this was my first real experience with a religious institution. The church, located in a small town in Northern California, considered itself "nondenominational," and the service usually consisted of a pastor reciting well-chosen biblical passages for about an hour and providing some minor inspirational interpretations. I attended sporadically, but needless to say, I was not moved by the experience and didn't take the idea of church seriously. Even though this doctrine was being force-fed to me for as long as I could remember, I always had questions about its veracity—questions that, I quickly learned, were considered inappropriate to ask.

I knew when I was six years old that my grandmother was a self-described traditional, God-fearing, Christian woman—it wasn't until much later, however, that I would realize the closed-mindedness that this mindset bred in her and others over time. She saw that I was not excited about attending church on a regular basis, and when I was around age eight, she mandated that I attend a weekly children's class at the same church in an attempt to force more involvement and encourage my participation within the "House of God." I remember my first day at this Sunday school very well; I recall that my younger stepsister was there with me in a classroom-like setting learning about Jesus Christ and his message, obviously at a superficial level that could be more easily absorbed by young children. I also remember the tactics utilized by the "teachers" to keep the attention of the children and get us excited about church—usually this consisted of giving gifts of candy and prizes for active participation. I do not doubt that the intentions of these people were positive, but in hindsight, I cannot help but see the gifts as a type of mild bribery in exchange for the willing indoctrination of a child. For instance, after we earned a certain amount of "Bible Bucks," which were awarded for correctly answering trivia questions about the Gospels and participating in Christian songs, we could cash in these vouchers for prizes like candy, toys, or even a ten-minute break to play on the trampoline behind the church.

The bus ride to and from Sunday school was the most exciting part of the event for my stepsister and me; we would play games and sing songs, and we were always given a lot of candy. My point in telling you this is not to glorify the practice of forcing a religion on a child before they reach the age of reason, but instead, my intention is to illuminate the ways in which this act is carried out within the Christian community and other religious traditions.

My stepsister was always excited to attend church for the prizes, and it didn't take long for this connection to become a subconscious one, which helped foster an extremely positive outlook of church and religion in her mind. For one reason or another, I did not have this reaction—I simply didn't take church or religion seriously. I remember thinking of it more as a pastime or a game to occupy my time on Sunday mornings, acknowledging that the "miracles" portrayed in the biblical texts could not have possibly occurred.

There is no point in my past in which I would have considered myself "Christian," or affiliated with any other religion, for that matter. But because my parents became increasingly religious over time and my grandparents had always taken Christianity as God's inherent truth, I was afraid to voice my opinions on the subject. It was this disparity between my family's faith and my naturalistic worldview that spurred my interest in the study of religion. It wasn't until age thirteen that I became interested in actively studying the various religious traditions in the world and their effects on society at large. It is because of this curiosity, and my sincere hope to avoid familial confrontation, that I decided to remain silent about my skepticism surrounding Christianity—and all religions. I continued to accompany my family to church on Sundays—as a silent observer. After years of attending the same Christian church nearly every week, however, I had a lot of unanswered questions about the religion's history and principles, and how it became the world's most followed religion. But out of fear of being ostracized, I remained silent and did not raise my specific concerns to my family, although my lack of participation and general attitude toward church was probably quite telling.

At age fifteen, long since having decided that I wasn't getting enough information out of the weekly sermons to justify any sort of divine revelation, I was determined to read the Bible in its entirety to get a more complete picture of what it teaches and, more importantly, why it teaches those things. It was at this time, after seeing firsthand the violent, discriminatory, and hate-filled passages that our pastor had neglected to read aloud every week, that I decided that not only was I not a Christian but that I was also against the notion of organized religion in general.

I could have remained silent for years as so many of us do, but instead I decided to confront my family head-on. It was at age fifteen that I first told my family that I didn't want to go to church anymore because I disagreed with the religion on a fundamental and moral level. I was honest and respectful about my opinions, but that didn't stop them from attempting to force my participation in the church—they probably thought they were doing the right thing, trying to "save my soul." I remember them being upset with me at first—as you might expect. But, because of my straightforward and honest attitude, and because I broached the subject rather early in life, it blew over relatively quickly. In short, they got over it. From age fifteen on, it was known to all those in my immediate family that I was a religious conscientious objector, and while some of the more closed-minded family members looked down on me for this rather bold announcement, I simply turned the other cheek. Now, I am an open atheist in my private and public lives and believe that I am truly better off for it. While keeping your opinions on issues related to dogma hidden might help to avoid small confrontations, being honest with yourself and others can be more rewarding in the long term. I truly empathize with those people who are still being forced to hide their non-religiosity from friends and family who might otherwise discriminate against them—and that's part of why I started this project.

I understand that, because I never fully believed in any deity or religion, my de-conversion and *coming out*—a phrase that's traditionally used by the LGBTQ community to refer to the moment an individual opens up about being LGBT or Q—isn't as divisive as some of my atheist friends and colleagues. Those who were more invested in church might have a more difficult time sharing their newfound skepticism with friends and family, who are likely enshrined in the same tradition—often with extreme fervor. This includes those nonbelievers who were once clergymen or preachers or otherwise associated with a religious tradition—this dynamic presents its own set of unique challenges.

But the reason my de-conversion was not a traumatic moment in my life is precisely because I didn't wait. By telling my family as soon as I was sure that I didn't want to be involved in the church, it became a soon-forgotten aspect to my developing personality—my family got used to it. By the time I was eighteen years old and I decided to attend school for religious studies, nobody in my family or circle of friends was surprised that I was interested in studying the phenomenon of religion from a secular perspective; and although I catch flak from strangers every once in a while, my true friends and family continue to love and respect me for who I am, regardless of our religious and ideological differences—of which there are many.

This is, in my opinion, how it can and should be for everybody, provided that all parties are honest with themselves and others and retain a respectful outlook. In this work, I will outline some steps to make the process easier for you and your loved ones to transition out of religion, provide testimonials from nonbelievers of all ages who decided to take the enormous step to become open about their atheism, and provide helpful information, resources, and support systems for all nonbelievers. The intention is that these instructions and stories will help people who are being forced to hide their thoughts and feelings from family and friends in a society largely dominated by religion, and to serve as a reference for those who have already come out as atheists. From dealing with grief from a secular perspective to handling potential clashes in religious worldviews between significant others or in the office, this guide offers multiple perspectives on how to deal with any situation, from nonreligious individuals who have generously donated their anecdotes to help those atheists in similar positions.

HI, I'M AN ATHEIST!

INTRODUCTION

> I contend that we are both atheists. I just
> believe in one fewer god than you do. When
> you understand why you dismiss all the other
> possible gods, you will understand why I
> dismiss yours.
>
> —STEPHEN F. ROBERTS

If you're reading this, it is likely that you've decided
that you don't believe. In a time period in which the
overwhelming majority of people not only believe in
god(s) but consider themselves religious in one form
or another, this can be an important, life-altering
decision. While some regions of the world are, as
a rule, less religious than others, the power of en-
culturation has always ensured the theistic majority's place in human society ahead of the others, and
being seen as nonreligious has long been the source
of negative actions and sentiments on the behalf of

religious groups. In fact, according to a 2011 study on anti-atheist prejudice sponsored by the American Psychological Association,* American and Canadian participants said they distrust atheists nearly as much as they distrust rapists when compared to Christians or Muslims.

In some areas of the world, a believer's knee-jerk reaction to one's non-religiosity alone can cause a traumatic situation or confrontation, and it is completely natural to have reservations about becoming an open atheist or, because of cultural stigmas, to consider yourself an atheist in the first place. While you may not believe in an all-knowing God or wish to be part of any organized religion, the term *atheist* has a negative connotation associated with it that has been historically difficult to overcome. To combat this, nonbelievers throughout history have created new monikers that could be used to display nonbelief in a more positive manner—without the baggage that is often associated with *atheist*. Some of these terms are: *bright, freethinker, (secular) humanist, nontheist, religiously unaffiliated, agnostic-atheist, skeptic, irreligionist, rationalist,* and *unbeliever.* Then there are those atheists who prefer to say they are "spiritual but

---

* Gervais, W. M., Shariff, A. F., & Norenzayan, A. (2011). "Do you believe in atheists? Distrust is central to anti-atheist prejudice," *Journal of Personality and Social Psychology,* 101(6), 1189–1206 https://doi.org/10.1037/a0025882.

not religious" or that they "just don't like organized religion." In many cases, these phrases are uttered by atheists who are afraid to say what they are, due to stigma or conditioning.

Although the term *atheist* may have begun as a derogatory or pejorative title, the literal meaning of "without god" or "a lack of belief in god(s)" remains important for our purposes, and I will continue to use *atheist* and *nonbeliever* to refer to a nonreligious person who is skeptical in regard to a supernatural Creator. An *open* atheist is a person who does not hide the fact that they don't participate in deity worship from their family, friends, and the general public. It is a common misconception that an atheist necessarily believes that the existence of a god or gods is impossible; the term simply refers to a person who doesn't believe that is the case. In other words, an atheist might simply believe that God, as a concept, is improbable. The definition of *God* also becomes increasingly important here. For *God* in this context, we will ascribe the semi-traditional definition of a supernatural Creator and/or Governor. This description applies to the proposed deities from a wide variety of religions and cultures, and an atheist is simply somebody who doubts the existence of such a being—no more, no less.

Some believers may try to assert that atheism is itself a religion, but this could not be further from the truth. "Atheism" can't be a religion because it's not a belief system—a lack of belief in a god or gods is the only commonality that all atheists share. I often have to remind believers that I don't pray to any idols, I don't believe in supernatural forces, I don't congregate with other atheists to worship atheism, and I don't tithe to an atheist "church."

The odds are that, if you are a closet atheist or a silent nonbeliever, your relatives or loved ones probably have a different approach to theological philosophies than you do—hence your hesitation in making your ideas public knowledge. Normally, familial disagreements in a broader sense would not be such an enormous problem, but when it comes to religious ideologies, specifically, the ideals and principles are often so firmly held and divisive that disagreements of this nature have been known to end an otherwise flourishing relationship. This is largely because most religions, and therefore most followers of those religions, presuppose the existence of a hell or hell-like afterlife in which "sinners" and nonbelievers reside after this life—as opposed to the supposed heaven or paradise where believers imagine they will be sent after death. Religions thrive on this mentality because it encourages proselytization and therefore the rapid spread of the tradition. As a result, the religious person far too often sees a nonbeliever, and instead of judging them based on their actions or simply not judging them at all, as most Abrahamic faiths instruct followers,* they see a sinner whose actions must be corrected to avoid burning in a lake of fire. If you're familiar with Christian teachings, for instance, you may be aware that it is often seen as a Christian's moral duty to share with the nonreligious the "Good Word" of God—and to save the person from an eternity in hell. That's part of how Christianity became so popular, by successfully permeating other cultures through missionary work, and other derived faiths share similar evangelical provisions.

Unfortunately, it is this same highly regarded concept of an afterlife that allows misguided religious people to justify the mistreatment of those who disagree with their religious ideologies—they are simply trying to protect you from eternal damnation in the afterlife by condemning you, insulting you, and even disowning you in this life.

This is not to say that becoming open about your disbelief is always going to be met with these negative reactions—and in fact, that is precisely what this work is hoping to prevent—but it is important to understand that if you experience negative reactions from religious kin, it is probably a result of the religion's teachings and

---

* Matthew 7:1–2 (NIV): "Do not judge, or you too will be judged. For in the same way you judge others, you will be judged, and with the measure you use, it will be measured to you."

likely not from any personal vendetta or hatred. Even just acknowledging that simple fact could make any negative response easier to comprehend and therefore handle.

The term *coming out* has been applied to the non-religious for years with great success, at least as early as August 2007 with the Out Campaign, which was popularized by noted evolutionary biologist Richard Dawkins and sought to let atheists know they aren't alone by encouraging individuals to come out and state their disbelief publicly. A group called Openly Secular was founded in 2014 with similar goals.

Although coming out as atheist has become commonplace, the term began in reference to homosexuals who disclose their sexual orientation to their family and friends—becoming "openly gay." This act, like becoming an open atheist, is often met with discrimination and familial misunderstanding at extreme levels and is often similarly associated with differing religious beliefs. Because most primary sects of the world's major religions condemn the act of homosexuality,* including fundamentalist Christianity and Islam, parents whose child's sexual orientation doesn't align with what is considered by their religion to be "moral" are forced to deal with the reality (as they perceive it) that their

---

* Leviticus 18:22 (NIV): "Do not have sexual relations with a man as one does with a woman; that is detestable."

child might suffer in hell for this behavior. There are a number of programs (sponsored by Christian churches or other religious organizations) that have seen tremendous financial success in preaching religion as the "cure" to homosexual behavior and that one can ensure a place in heaven by "praying the gay away." Of course, these "conversion therapy" programs do not work and have been linked to depression, suicidality, anxiety, social isolation, and decreased capacity for intimacy, according to a study analysis from Cornell University.* In the everyday life of a newly public atheist, this mentality might be translated into the onslaught of religious literature and church invitations that often occur once an atheist has made their lack of religious convictions open and available to loved ones. The parallels between these two concepts of revelation are numerous, which is why the expression *coming out* will come up again as applied to atheism.

It is often difficult for a person who was raised in a religious tradition to deny the teachings they have known since childhood to such an extent that they no longer identify with them—and wish this to be known

---

* "What Does the Scholarly Research Say About Whether Conversion Therapy Can Alter Sexual Orientation Without Causing Harm?," Cornell University, https://whatweknow .inequality.cornell.edu/topics/lgbt-equality/what-does-the -scholarly-research-say-about-whether-conversion-therapy-can -alter-sexual-orientation-without-causing-harm/.

to others. It is even more difficult for someone to take an active stance against the ideologies or systems taught since childhood—not because the religious arguments are especially convincing or transcendent but because of the indoctrination that inherently takes place within a religious tradition.

Some who are involved in church on a deeper level might also fear political pressures to keep their disbelief a secret. In the United States, the majority of atheists probably come from a more liberal religious background, for the simple reason that most American Christians practice a form of cultural Christianity, in that they inherit the traditions but don't necessarily understand or care about the intricacies of the religion. To expand upon the cultural aspects of religiosity, I'd like to quote an essay, entitled "Cultural Christianity," which was published in my first book, *Disproving Christianity and Other Secular Writings**:

> I am referring to a phenomenon that I came across during the course of my research that, to me, demonstrates that religion can be something similar to heritage in that it is passed on from generation to generation through the parents.
>
> For example, people who have extremely limited

---

* David G. McAfee, *Disproving Christianity and Other Secular Writings,* 3rd ed., revised, (n.p.: Hypatia Press, 2019), 2.

knowledge of the Bible or its implications may still choose to classify themselves as "Christians" on the basis that their parents did so. This phenomenon of children inheriting religion is often overlooked because the perpetrator guilty of indoctrination is not a dictator or cult leader, but their own parents. When a child is growing up, there is a crucial period in which they begin to ask questions about the origin of existence—in a religious family, these questions are typically answered [in accordance with] . . . church or Sunday school. Once these beliefs are instilled in the child, it becomes a part of his or her identity—so much so that, in many cases, the child will grow up and forever identify him- or herself with that specific religion without question or skepticism.

While a religious person may disagree with the term *indoctrination* in this context, I would argue that it is especially apt for the discussion of religious instruction of children. Contrary to popular belief, indoctrination itself does not imply any negative intentions or motivations; it simply means that somebody instructs with a bias in regard to a particular doctrine or ideology (usually in reference to a child).* By taking a child to church and

---

* *Merriam-Webster,* s.v. "indoctrinate," http://www.merriam-webster.com/dictionary/indoctrinate.

teaching them that the rules and ideas learned there are legitimate and sacred, saying prayers in the home, and teaching the validity of religious scriptures (even when they sometimes conflict with modern scientific findings), it is exactly this in which most religious families participate. I'd go as far as to say that most believers, whether they are Christian, Muslim, Hindu, or something else, would probably admit that they instruct their children with a bias toward their particular faith.

After being exposed to this indoctrination, as most of us are in one form or another, a religion often becomes as firmly held in us as it is in those who raised us, leading to a cycle of similar indoctrination. One rarely questions what they have always known to be reality. It is only once a person begins to ask questions regarding the validity of these inherited traditions that they can break free from the cycle of indoctrination and, occasionally, experience a secular breakthrough within a family otherwise inclined toward religion. In some cases, the result is a nonbeliever who is surrounded by religious loved ones with whom they would like to share their thoughts and concerns, but can't for fear of discrimination and other negative reactions.

It isn't just familial honesty and transparency that the nonreligious have to deal with in daily life, however. Even those of us whose family members are mainly nonreligious, non-present, or otherwise supportive have to deal with coming out as a nonbeliever in public life with friends, coworkers, and even strangers. In fact, coming out as a nonreligious individual should not be thought of as a onetime occurrence but an ongoing event in which one must continually decide whether or not to speak openly about their rejection of faith with people with whom they interact. While it is often considered general etiquette to not discuss politics or religion in order to preserve personal and professional relationships, this does not mean that the topic never arises. And it is possible that a religious person presupposes religiosity in conversation and thereby forces the nonbeliever to either confirm or deny their assumptions. Coming out as an atheist can also apply to these interactions. The notion that informing your family that you are not religious is the entirety of the difficulty with coming out as an atheist could not be further from the truth. Some people choose to remain silenter in the public sphere in regard to religious preferences, which is completely acceptable and understandable. But it is also true that you shouldn't be forced to hide your lack of religious ideologies—and having such open discourse shouldn't necessitate a confrontational interaction.

After all, why does your lack of religious fervor have to be a source of controversy? Does it actually affect anybody but you in any real way? The fact that you don't see sufficient evidence to cultivate a belief in a supernatural Creator, which they happen to believe in, should not be a point of disagreement that leads to an inability to get along or to have comfortable interactions. In fact, many would argue, as I have in the past, that "atheism" is the default human setting—as you are not born with knowledge of gods; it is simply from living and being introduced to the concept that a believer adopts theism. At the end of the day, your personal feelings and beliefs surrounding religion don't impact the well-being of anybody else, and you shouldn't be afraid to be as honest as possible with yourself and others about that fact. Hopefully, this guide will allow you to do just that, while maintaining your positive personal relationships with loved ones.

2

WHY SHOULD I COME OUT?

It was a high counsel that I once heard given
to a young person, "Always do what you are
afraid to do."

—RALPH WALDO EMERSON,
AMERICAN ESSAYIST

Coming out as an atheist can be scary. In some instances, it can be one of the most difficult things to
do; not only are you telling your family that everything
they've instilled in you since childhood is bunk, but you
are telling them that you choose to disassociate yourself from religious belief altogether. Nonetheless, coming out is usually necessary and always something to
carefully consider prior to committing. Overly religious
family members and fears of possible bigotry and discrimination might intimidate you, but it is important
to remember that the only way to fight such discrimination is to shatter the misconceptions about atheism and

secularism that currently exist in society. According to the 2007 Pew Forum on Religion and Public Life, only 1.6 percent of the thirty-five thousand respondents described themselves as "atheist," although 6.3 percent described themselves as "secular unaffiliated" and 2.4 percent as agnostic. There is certainly a great deal more than 1.6 percent atheists in the United States, but only by people coming out and being open about their atheism can that be more accurately represented. Still, there are scenarios in which coming out is not the right choice. Individuals growing up in fundamentalist denominations of Islam and Christianity, for instance, may experience direct threats to their lives or livelihood as a result of being open about their atheism. In those cases, the issue isn't as clear.

Religious traditions often use the idea that you are somehow a sinner since birth to guilt you into believing, while the truth is that you were probably a great person to begin with. So why should being an "atheist" change anything? In many cases, it is because believers often see atheism as "against god." Negative associations with secularism go back as far as religious belief itself; in modern and ancient religions, nonbelievers are often represented as the "enemy." By being open about the fact that you're unconvinced by religions, you can show that atheism is not a result of "demons" or "Satan" or any other "evil" thing, but instead it is the result of thinking and research and reason. You can help add to a growing minority of openly atheist individuals bound together by nothing more than one thing: a lack of belief in gods.

By telling people you don't believe, you're making it a bit easier for the next person who has to. You are making it that much easier for the next generation and helping to change the (very false) perception of atheism as something that is anti-god or even pro-evil. More than anything else, coming out as an atheist gives you the opportunity to educate believers—to show them that it is entirely possible to be morally good without believing that we are being policed by an all-knowing deity.

Another reason to come out? Honesty. While some people are so fundamentally stuck in their beliefs that they will hate you for disagreeing, the vast majority of believers and nonbelievers alike are comfortable with some level of disagreement, and when conditions are ideal, they can usually agree to disagree. People often appreciate truth over deceit, so if you are attempting to avoid confrontation, honesty is the best policy.

In some cases, your loved ones will understand that it is natural to disagree, and they may even welcome friendly debate. But even when there is familial tension, it rarely exceeds the downsides of remaining silent. Just by allowing people to assume you are religious (which they undoubtedly will, considering the presence of a religious majority in many areas) does a great disservice to the larger secular community by downplaying how many atheists there actually are. While atheists are larger than some other minority groups, they are for the most part non-present in the political domain in many nations, including and especially the United States.

There is a lot of debate and argument about the word *atheist*. Some people are so inherently turned off by the word that they seek alternatives, including misapplying titles like *agnostic*—a term that is not mutually exclusive with *atheist* and in fact speaks to an entirely different issue. While atheism is about belief, agnosticism is about knowledge. Another misconception about atheism is that it somehow means someone denies even the very possibility of a deity. In all actuality, it simply means you don't believe it to be the case—a point that should not be hard to understand with the complete lack of physical evidence that points to the existence of such a being or beings. Even if you're 51 percent sure that there is no magical man in the sky, you are an atheist; and admitting that is the first half of the battle.

3

ATHEIST ACTIVIST WITH AN AXE TO GRIND

Prejudice, not being founded on reason, cannot be removed by argument.

—SAMUEL JOHNSON, ENGLISH WRITER

Being an open atheist since a very young age, I never hid the fact that I didn't believe. For that reason, I believe I have the ability to show through my experiences the good and bad that comes with being an atheist in a society largely intolerant of non-religiosity. The negative experience to which I'm referring came in the form of discrimination against my atheist activism when applying for the graduate program for religious studies at the University of California–Santa Barbara (UCSB) in November of 2010.

I studied at UCSB for four years, coming to the campus directly out of high school at age eighteen. I majored in religious studies and English, and I never had any issue with my lack of religious beliefs in any of my courses.

To clarify, I majored in religious studies, the study of religions from a phenomenological approach, which is not to be confused with Christian theology—the study of Christianity as a fundamental truth. I distinctly remember having a few professors who advocated for the position of one religion or another, but I had never been discriminated against for not believing. As graduation grew near, I decided that I wanted to pursue my education in religious studies at UCSB in the form of the RGST graduate program and master's/PhD program, having had a successful and enjoyable tenure there during my undergraduate years. We learned about the historical and cultural aspects of various religions—in some cases even drawing the rightful parallels between the creation myths of the Greeks and Native American and Hindu traditions and those of Abrahamic and Judeo-Christian religions. Although I am not a religious person and, in fact, oppose religion in its extremer and more violent forms, I find the historical and comparative aspects of religious studies extremely helpful in understanding how the human mind works and why people believe the things that they do, which is why I've studied religion since a very young age. At a public university like UCSB and in a nation bound by a separation of church and state like the United States of America, this course of study should be acceptable for somebody of any or no faith, or so I thought.

Prior to submitting my application for the MA/PhD program, I was recommended by an adviser to contact

A. T., a professor of religious studies and chair of the committee handling graduate-level applications for the department. I was instructed to set up a meeting with her in order to "put a face to my application." I had taken two classes with her in the past but hadn't had any significant interactions, positive or negative, so I figured it couldn't hurt my chances. I did as I was told and set up the meeting via email and met with her a week later.

When I walked in the door to her office, A. T. seemed friendly enough. She asked me about my aspirations, and I told her that I wanted to be a writer and that I had self-published a book the year before. I didn't mention whether or not the work had been related to my studies, nor did I imply that its content was relevant to my application within the department. Upon hearing that I had a book published, A. T. turned to her computer and immediately googled my name; the first result was my Amazon.com page for my first book: *Disproving Christianity: Refuting the World's Most Followed Religion.** I could see her computer monitor, and while I was a little bit nervous, I was sure that writing a book of compiled biblical criticisms in my spare time couldn't be used against me—especially because this work was completely separate from my UCSB course studies. I was wrong. A. T. turned to me and said, "I need to word this carefully. You wouldn't fit in with

---

* David G. McAfee, *Disproving Christianity: Refuting the World's Most Followed Religion* (n.p.: CreateSpace, 2010).

our department's milieu because you are an atheist activist with an axe to grind." I was stunned. I told her that the assumption was a ridiculous one, and I even posed the rebuttal that a Christian who had done missionary work would certainly not be denied because of that fact—and I'd say a missionary is at least as much of an activist as I am. Sure enough, a few weeks later, my application was denied. Whether or not this interaction was the reason for the rejection, A. T.'s behavior was inappropriate, unprofessional, and illegal.

It was these words, coupled with her refusal to apologize when I confronted her in person and by email, that led me to seek justice—if not within the university, then in public opinion. I wrote the article "Atheist Activist with an Axe to Grind" and received plenty of criticism by Christians who said that, as an atheist, I shouldn't be studying religion in the first place. But more importantly, I received numerous messages in support of my cause, and the article was picked up by popular atheist websites, including *Friendly Atheist*,* and was even mentioned by *The Washington Post*.**

---

* "Atheist Rejected from Grad School Because of His Activism?," *Friendly Atheist,* April 13, 2011, http://www.patheos.com/blogs/friendlyatheist/2011/04/30/atheist-rejected-from-grad-school-because-of-his-activism/.
** Herb Silverman, "Why Do Americans Still Hate Atheists? Herb Silverman Explains," *Washington Post,* May 4, 2011, http://

Readers wrote letters of support to the school and to the vice chancellor of student affairs for UCSB, who approached me and asked me what I hoped to gain from this. I didn't anticipate the meeting that followed, but I was happy that the people who read my story felt inspired enough to defend religious freedoms in a public sphere.

Clearly, with this incident of religious intolerance, I lost my appetite for continued enrollment with UCSB in any fashion, so a secondary review of my application or admission into the program would not suffice to make up for the discriminatory comments by A. T. And although I maintain that the professor's actions were illegal, I did not seek to defame the campus by taking my case to trial as a result of one administrator's behavior. Instead, I asked for the one thing that could demonstrate that the religious studies department would not tolerate this type of behavior in the future and showed acknowledgment and recognition of the error. I wanted to be sure that nonreligious students who enjoy studying religion would not be discriminated against in this way, so I asked for a formal letter of apology from the head of the religious studies department at UCSB, José Cabezón.

---

live.washingtonpost.com/why-do-americans-hate-atheists-herb
-silverman.html.

Less than a month later, thanks to the many letters of support sent to the religious studies department on my behalf, and after an extensive investigation by the UCSB Office of Student Affairs, I received just such a letter. It stated the following:

> *I am writing on behalf of the Religious Studies department to apologize for any comments that may have been made by Professor [A. T.] during a conversation you had with her on November 23, 2010, about your interest in UCSB's graduate program in Religious Studies. While I was not present during that conversation, I want to assure you that it is the firm policy of the Religious Studies department not to discriminate against applicants on the basis of religious beliefs or lack thereof. If Professor [A. T.] implied otherwise, then this was inappropriate. Issues of religious beliefs, activism, or activities unrelated to one's own academic work should not be considerations in the admissions process.*

Now that the ordeal is over, I've decided to attend graduate school elsewhere after taking some time to work as a journalist and publish this and other written works. I've also since republished my first book in a revised third edition. But I am happy with the outcome of the investigation, and I hope this small victory might help those nonbelievers who might be discriminated against based merely on the fact that they don't believe. Thank you to everybody who supported me through letters to the university on my behalf.

4

WHAT DOES IT MEAN TO BE AN ATHEIST?

Atheism leaves a man to sense, to philosophy, to natural piety, to laws, to reputation; all of which may be guides to an outward moral virtue, even if religion vanished; but religious superstition dismounts all these and erects an absolute monarchy in the minds of men.

—FRANCIS BACON,
PHILOSOPHER AND STATESMAN

As an openly nonreligious individual, you will no doubt receive reactions to your lack of religiosity ranging from genuine curiosity to blind and hateful criticism. In short, you will need to be prepared to answer an onslaught of questions regarding what you believe, why you believe it, and even if and when you were "de-converted." To answer some of these ideological questions that apply to the nature of atheism, I've put together a small description of exactly what it means to be an atheist or sub-scribe to a secular worldview. Oftentimes, identifying yourself as an atheist is harder than the initial rejection of the dogma itself, largely because of the negative cultural connotations that have plagued the community. This chapter will help to destroy some of the common misconceptions associated with *atheist*.

The most commonly asked question toward non-believers on behalf of believers, in my opinion, is regarding any ultimate "goal" or reality present within a secular individual's mindset. "If not for God and religion, what point is there to it all?" they might ask. I generally respond to this type of inquiry by stating that, as an atheist, I don't claim to know an overar-ching "meaning of life," but I do operate under the understanding that life should not be lived under the pretense that it is simply a "test" propagated by an invisible, intangible Creator-God. And it should not be spent identifying with religious traditions and organized groups that, historically, have been at the root of a tremendous amount of oppression and vio-lence. It is my sincere opinion that our precious time on earth should not be spent attempting to justify unbelievable acts of cruelty, death, and disease as a part of "God's plan" or the greater good—and cling-ing to ancient texts that preach ill-concealed bigotry and sexism. Instead, we should find ways to make this life happy and satisfying for ourselves as well as other beings, without regard to the unknowable nature of an afterlife. After all, as Marcus Aurelius once said:

> *Live a good life. If there are gods and they are just, then they will not care how devout you have been, but will welcome you based on the virtues you have lived by. If there are gods, but unjust, then you should not want to worship them. If there are no gods, then you will be gone, but will have lived a noble life that will live on in the memories of your loved ones.**

In the Christian tradition, according to John 14:6** and other biblical passages, a requirement for passage into heaven is that you accept the Lord Jesus Christ as your savior. From this fact, a few questions immediately spring to mind:

Would a truly fair, merciful, and just Creator really condemn those individuals who have never heard of Jesus or even those of us who have heard the name Jesus Christ, yet see no physical or historical evidence to warrant belief?

Shouldn't someone be forgiven for simply being born into a different religion with a different god?

---

* Quote by Marcus Aurelius, Roman emperor (April 26, 121–March 17, 180).
** John 14:6 (NIV): "Jesus answered, 'I am the way and the truth and the life. No one comes to the Father except through me.'"

Should it be enough to simply be the best person you can be? According to the Christian Gospel, the answer is simply—and firmly—*no*.*

These questions can be similarly applied to several other religions, including most interpretations of Islam. In Islam, there is a requirement to believe in Allah or be sent to hell, which is also called Jahannam.

In addition to answering a believer's questions, it doesn't hurt to ask a few of your own that might make your stance on religion more easily understood. "What makes you think your God is the right one?" is an especially important question to ask any believer, as it might help one realize their own cultural ties to their specific religious beliefs. In fact, there are thousands of proposed gods and goddesses with similar stories and myths that supposedly link them to reality—the Judeo-Christian God is no exception. Each religious canon has its own fallacies and contradictions that we have outgrown scientifically over time, yet the outlooks of these religions have continued to adapt and evolve with human society and morality, attempting (often without success) to discard the archaic principles within holy texts as symbolism or metaphor as the religion is handed down generation by generation through familial instructions. To prevent myself from unintentionally identifying with any of these flawed traditions, I

---

* Thessalonians 1:8.

consider myself a *naturalist* and a *rationalist* above all other ideologies. This means that I do not believe in any gods, devils, angels, talking snakes, ghosts, vampires, or any other supernatural beings. That does make me an atheist, but that is not how I'd identify myself foremost. I simply utilize scientific evidence and common sense to form opinions based on the best information available to me. I do this without relying on traditional and familial influences to make my decisions or encourage the invention of supernatural beings or forces to assign meaning or attempt to explain the unknown. Few believers acknowledge the statistical assumption that, had they been born to another family in a different culture, they would likely have had equally strong faith in another god or multiple gods . . . I would still be a naturalist because I've personally never seen evidence that justifies belief in anything supernatural. I am, of course, open to changing my mind with evidence.

Religion has been used to accomplish an enormous number of goals throughout history, both positive and negative. But these negative impacts remain, in my opinion, unjustifiable in the long run: from justifying the oppression of women and lower-class citizens to being the motivation and/or catalyst for some of the brutalest of wars, the mentality that one group understands a god's wishes and can act upon them has historically been a practice of various religious traditions since their inception. It is especially true that government officials, including in the "secular" United States, adopt the idea that their "God" is somehow rooting for them, and then employ it in warfare.

Although religion has motivated violence and has long been the source of scientific restriction and regress, the origin of religious beliefs is, in almost all cases, a crutch for providing an explanation for the otherwise inexplicable. As a student of religious studies looking at the origins of all sorts of religious traditions, it was abundantly clear to me that the earliest "religions" (more accurately, worship rituals) were created not out of hatred or bias but out of ignorance combined with our human desire to do away with it or conceal it from ourselves.

The "God of the Gaps" is an idea for which we, as modern humans who have a basic understanding of and appreciation for science, have little to no use, since scientific discoveries have shown us how the earth came to be, how humanity evolved from our primitive ancestors, where the sun goes at night, and how viruses spread—leaving little room for the outdated religious explanations for these so-called phenomena and miracles. In a modern paradigm, religious precepts and spirituality are adopted as a concept for the purposes of dealing with grief, fear of the unknown, and a sense of community and higher purpose.

All in all, I'm not one to dispute the therapeutic value of spirituality, and I've seen religious traditions provide comfort to those who seek it out in times of great distress. However, mysticism and spirituality have never provided something that secular therapies, which don't come with the psychological baggage of religions, could not offer. Those people who claim to need religion to cope with the realities of day-to-day life—or to justify their morality—could not be further from the truth in most cases. In fact, for those individuals, a religion may provide a sense of well-being in an otherwise overwhelming world, but it rarely leads people to solve their problems; it often only encourages them to leave these issues up to the mystical higher power and dodge responsibility. This has been seen, for instance, in some implementations of the twelve-step recovery programs based on Alcoholics Anonymous and Narcotics Anonymous. As part of that process, participants (even nonbelievers) are asked to accept that they can't change certain things and leave parts of their lives up to an undefined higher power. It's easy to see how this mentality, if taken to its extremes, could lead a person toward inaction in their daily lives in lieu of petitionary prayer.

While this tactic may give the appearance of resolution to the believer, it is difficult to justify such an action in light of the loss of individual accomplishments and spirit. It is when the principles of religion begin to be taken too seriously at a fundamental level, to the point of extremes, that it becomes no longer therapeutic but harmful to society and the individual. This happens when people leave things entirely up to a deity or when they begin to act on that god's behalf to motivate their own ambitions, as well as any time a person's priority is shifted from the important issues of the known temporal world to the faith-based belief in the next.

5

HOW CAN I BE GOOD WITHOUT GOD?

> With or without religion, you would have good people doing good things and evil people doing evil things. But for good people to do evil things, that takes religion.
>
> —STEVEN WEINBERG,
> NOBEL LAUREATE IN PHYSICS

One reason that a religious person might give for having issues with your de-conversion from religion to a more naturalistic understanding of the world is that many religions propose themselves as the one unified source of an objective morality. In other words, they teach that "moral living," altruism, and general goodness are impossible without their god(s) and the holy scriptures that support them. According to the Christian tradition, for example, the texts assert that it is impossible to be moral without accepting Jesus "into your heart."* In Islam, while there are a number of prescriptions for showing kindness, giving to charity anonymously, and forgiving others, the term for morality is closely linked to love for Allah and Allah's creatures. As an open nonbeliever, it will be useful to be able to explain that this is simply not the case. Not only is it possible to be good without God—but, I would argue, it is much easier.

The concept of a transcendent, divine morality that is unattainable without living in accordance with a specific religion is a flawed idea for two major reasons. Firstly, we can see how moral values could have evolved (and likely did) over time within society in conjunction with the evolution of other social constructs, such as a sense of community, nationalism, and even democracy. Secondly, it is easily shown that altruism is a uniquely nonreligious concept once morality and worship are distinguished from one another—as they rarely are in religious institutions. I think that what we now call "morality" has evolved—as nearly all social and physical human attributes have—to aid us in survival and, ultimately, reproduction. This morality requires that we be guided only by a conscience (or "moral sense") and not by a god or gods.

---

* Most Christians would argue that everyone is born a sinner and will be punished as such unless the individual accepts belief in Jesus Christ.

The evolution of morality can be thought about in similar terms to physical evolution. We can determine which aspects of our ancestors' behaviors best allowed for the primitive communities to flourish—therefore ensuring that those behaviors flourished in future generations and remain present (and continually changing) to this day. Charles Darwin's theory of evolution by natural selection can be used to explain many of the otherwise inexplicable traits of modern humans, from mate selection to social interactions and even child-rearing. What many people don't realize, however, is that the same logic can also explain the sense of morality among humans in the absence of a theological (and therefore supernatural) definition.

Our understanding of what is moral is always changing. For example, until a few hundred years ago, it would have been perfectly morally acceptable to own and sell human beings as slaves. Yet today, this practice is condemned as, many would argue, universally immoral—of course, this does not mean that all areas of the world have adapted to this more modern viewpoint. Perhaps most importantly, the Bible still condones such behavior, and it always will. The same goes for the mistreatment of women and those individuals considered "lesser" socially—ideas that are prevalent in many religions, including and especially within the texts of the Abrahamic faiths.

This development, progression, and fluidity of cultural ethics and norms is precisely what makes the Bible a poor, stagnant, moral compass for today's society. Not only does the Holy Bible condone acts that our modern society would find completely unethical, such as rape, murder, and slavery, but it also condemns acts like homosexual orientation in the New Testament and wearing mixed-fabric clothing and working on Sundays in the Old Testament—acts that, today, could be considered normal and completely separate from "morality."

The fact is humans are social animals by nature, much like some other primates in the animal kingdom; it is only natural that, to live and thrive in a society, there is some level of cooperation among the members of the group. This basic, evolutionary certainty is what undoubtedly led to the eventual formation of what is "moral" and what is not. If our ancestors had not realized the importance of communal cooperation, they may have become a weaker species that wouldn't have survived on a long-term time line. In other words, if it had been beneficial to our primitive common ancestors to murder one's own family members, have incestuous relationships from which less capable children could be born, or act outside of societal expectations, humanity, as it exists today, may not have become a reality.

To ensure that others in the society followed the same ethical values, social contracts may have—at one time—not been enough. And promising eternal damnation or rewards in the afterlife based on behavior in this life was probably a useful way to keep people in line—in addition to the obvious benefits of dissuading revolution from the oppressed. But today, in the modern world, our values have grown and groups advocating for religious morality have become opposed to contemporary morality—such groups include religious extremists like the Ku Klux Klan, jihadists, Crusaders, Nazis, and antiabortion terrorist organizations, among others. We have in place a system, however, in which people are employed by the government to investigate, arrest, prosecute, and detain offenders based on the violation of laws that are as fluid as our cultural ideals and established by humans, and not humans posing as gods—and can be amended as such. While certainly not perfect, this legal system has developed over time to ensure one's accordance with rules and regulations that are not considered to be permanent or divine; this eliminates the need for a supernatural punishment/reward system based on an afterlife—like those often presented in ancient holy texts that feed on the gullibility and fear of people seeking something more than this life.

In the Christian tradition, the concept of morality is tied directly to pleasing the Judeo-Christian God; this is evident in the presence of God-serving attributes listed as the first, second, third, and fourth of the worshipped Ten Commandments present in Exodus and Deuteronomy. This means that nearly half of the Ten Commandments that were supposedly given directly from God to Moses to guide moral living on earth are directed toward serving God, worshipping God, and preventing "other gods" from encroaching on "His" domain. The first four commandments don't condemn rape or slavery or bigotry—in fact, those concepts are conveniently absent from the Commandments entirely. Here are the divine, transcendent, moral goods as established in Exodus of the New King James Bible:

> *I am the Lord your God, who brought you out of the land of Egypt, out of the house of bondage. You shall have no other gods before Me.*
>
> *You shall not make for yourself a carved image, or any likeness of anything that is in heaven above, or that is in the earth beneath, or that is in the water under the earth; you shall not bow down to them nor serve them. For I, the Lord your God, am a jealous God, visiting the iniquity of the fathers on the children to the third and fourth generations of those who hate Me, but showing mercy to thousands, to those who love Me and keep My Commandments.*
>
> *You shall not take the name of the Lord your God in vain, for the Lord will not hold him guiltless who takes His name in vain.*
>
> *Remember the Sabbath day, to keep it holy. Six days you shall labor and do all your work, but the seventh day is the Sabbath of the Lord your God. In*

it you shall do no work: you, nor your son, nor your daughter, nor your male servant, nor your female servant, nor your cattle, nor your stranger who is within your gates. For in six days the Lord made the heavens and the earth, the sea, and all that is in them, and rested the seventh day. Therefore the Lord blessed the Sabbath day and hallowed it.

Honor your father and your mother, that your days may be long upon the land which the Lord your God is giving you.

You shall not murder.

You shall not commit adultery.

You shall not steal.

You shall not bear false witness against your neighbor.

You shall not covet your neighbor's house; you shall not covet your neighbor's wife, nor his male servant, nor his female servant, nor his ox, nor his donkey, nor anything that is your neighbor's.

In most major religions, moral living is tied to belief, which makes a nonbeliever inherently amoral from that religion's perspective. This fact makes the explanation of secular morality even more important when coming out as an atheist to friends and family. A religious person might hear that you are no longer religious and auto-

---

* Exodus 20:2–17 (NKJV).

matically associate that concept with "sin" or immoral behaviors when, in fact, true altruism is only possible without a theological understanding of goodness. Altruism is defined as a principle of unselfish concern for the welfare of others.* In other words, an altruistic action is doing "good" for others only for the sake of the helpful act itself; this is to say that there are no ulterior motives. In this sense, not only do I think that it is possible to maintain moral standards without the crutch of religion, but I would argue that it is the only way to achieve true goodness and altruism. Free from the constraints of organized religion, a human being is able to express decency from one's self—as opposed to attempting to appease whatever higher power they may believe in. By separating worship and morality, we can act in accordance with our own human ethics and are able to be less selfish in our motivations for kindness and moral behaviors. To me, that makes a big difference.

---

* *Merriam-Webster,* s.v. "altruism," http://www.merriam-webster .com/dictionary/altruism.

6

TIMING IS EVERYTHING

You can create something that is pure genius,
but you have to get your timing right.

—LANG LEAV, NOVELIST AND POET

As is the case with most major decisions in life, timing could be one of the most important factors when coming out as a nonbeliever to your family and friends. If deciding to tell your loved ones about your de-conversion is the first step, then timing the delivery is the second. Planning can prove to be immensely helpful in this area in that a spontaneous, off-the-cuff announcement—through an argument, for example—can catch your family off guard, leaving you and your loved ones unprepared. When dealing with religious family members, coming out as an atheist has an even greater potential to end in rejection and pain; so, in these situations, planning an early, logical, and considerate approach to sharing your de-conversion from religion is the most important part of the process.

When it comes to coming out, the simplest piece of advice I can give is, "The earlier the better." Religious family members may be upset to hear about your departure from faith in the tradition that they practice, but time will always help those who truly love you understand and accept that their religion simply doesn't reach the burden of proof necessary to warrant lifelong dedication—in your opinion and the opinions of countless others; after all, "time heals all wounds." The time it often takes family members to understand this change is exactly why planning to express your doubts in religious institutions as early as you begin having them is such an important element in any transition to becoming openly nonreligious—and making sure that your doubts are not misunderstood. It is interesting to note that, from a religious perspective, doubt and skepticism of faith is often cast as "God testing you," or "the devil tricking you," or some variant, whereas it is much likelier that your critical-thinking skills are starting to make headway.

This is not to say that the first time you question religion you should immediately tell your family that you're an atheist, but openly expressing doubt may help plant the seeds with more "traditional" family members for a future naturalistic revelation. What it does mean is that, if you are sure that you want to share your secularism with your family and friends, then the earlier you make the information known, the earlier they can solve their own issues with your de-conversion that stem from their own insecurities in faith-based religions and accept your choices, hopefully ensuring everyone's happiness. Disassociation with a given religious system does not have to be a devastating familial interaction; often, as is the case within my own family, sharing your secular mentality as early as possible can help loved ones get used to the idea and prevent major impacts in the future of your relationships. In short, as long as you take a healthy approach to sharing your de-conversion, they will usually get over it—it is just a matter of time.

For those who have been hiding behind an image of religiosity, timing can also refer to the literal time you choose to let the world know that you are no longer going to blindly follow ancient man-made scripture—that is, in relation to other familial situations and interactions. By this I mean that it is important to plan a specific—and comfortable—time to be honest with your loved ones. As you might expect, it is usually considered bad form to come out in an argument about religion—and it is certainly in poor taste to purposefully belittle someone else's beliefs in the process. As was discussed earlier, for some people, there are therapeutic benefits for believing in something "greater" than mankind, so it is important not to judge them for their beliefs—just as it is important for them not to judge you based on your lack thereof. This type of confrontational behavior will ensure that your message is delivered to family in a time of stress or tension and will subsequently convey those negative feelings; in most cases, that only serves to make the acceptance process more difficult for you and your family in the long run. When you finally decide to show your skepticism toward your religious tradition, it is also important to remember that your religious friends and family members have probably held these belief systems for many years and they were most likely engrained in them as young children—you cannot expect them to suddenly realize the error of their ways and give up on religious mythology without significant thought and self-discovery. These are beliefs that have been flourishing and fortifying in some cases since childhood and today may provide comfort for those who fear the unknown or even retain a fear of purposelessness in a more general sense, and they will not be easily shaken. Nor is it your responsibility to de-convert them; instead, think of it as your obligation to present your opinions in a logical manner, educate loved ones on your motives for separating from religion if prompted, and love your family no matter what they choose to believe in or disregard; after all, it is a person's actions that define them—and not their belief system or their atheism.

The act of being honest with those for whom you care deeply regarding your thoughts and opinions on "divine" matters should be a celebratory one. The sheer willpower it takes to break away from the cultural constructs that were (in many cases) enforced in your psyche as a child is impressive in itself, and risking familial pain and disappointment in the spirit of truth and transparency is even more commendable. Support is what you need more than ever, but some believers who care for you might see this transitional period as one of confusion and "sin"—one that they are sometimes ill-equipped to handle. It is often the case that, in these instances, a de-conversion is met with anger and sadness as a result of instinctual and reactive behavior on behalf of the loved ones who once showed nothing but respect and admiration. This is not because religion makes people inherently bad or corrupt; it seems likelier the case that they are simply set in their ways and without the support system necessary to deal with such a shock to the cultural norms to which they have grown accustomed. Just as you need the support of your family to know that you won't be disowned for disputing theistic claims, your family may need support to know what this means for them and their faith. Having a concerned and religious loved one talk to a religious leader might help console them—depending on what that leader chooses to represent to them—but most often it helps to involve other family members who are supportive or otherwise able to help mediate the interaction between yourself and your more fundamentally religious kin. In the Resources and Support section, I will provide a helpful directory of organizations and communities that provide much-needed support for former believers and their family members.

For those parents who did everything in their power to ensure the realization of a pious and God-fearing child, finding out that they are nonreligious can be a shock to the system. This, however, is no excuse to keep your feelings on faith a secret from your loved ones; dishonesty does not build personal relationships. In fact, hiding the truth often aids in the destruction of these relationships. And letting them know that you do love them—and therefore your honesty with them is of the utmost importance to you—can be an easy way to break the tension between you and your theistic relatives. The planning of the event itself can be liberating on its own, not to mention the confidence one gains from a successful "revelation" after which your ultimate goal is realized: receipt of support and validation of your loved ones for simply being you—without prejudices or discrimination based on belief or lack of belief. It is not uncommon that the fact that one has gone through so much trouble to share one's dismissal of faith with their loved ones in a supportive and organized manner actually demonstrates to loved ones how important their familial opinions really are. This sometimes spurs the beginning stages of the acceptance process on its own, and the power of this concept should not be underestimated.

7

CONFRONTATION

A man is accepted into a church for what he believes and he is turned out for what he knows.

—SAMUEL CLEMENS (MARK TWAIN),
AMERICAN WRITER

Confrontation is a natural part of any interaction involving a member of a family dissenting from the others, especially when it comes to the topic of religion or politics. But on a more fundamental level, confrontation results from these religious discussions for a bigger reason: you're telling them that their most fundamental beliefs are wrong.

In many cases, religious beliefs are firmly held ideas that have been reinforced since an incredibly young age. When you tell someone—even if it is a family member or close friend—that you don't believe in their God, a defensive reaction isn't surprising. Oftentimes, you're telling them that everything they've ever known, everything their parents and their childhood idols ever told them, is wrong. For some nonbelievers who used to be active within a religious institution, this point is well understood. Letting go of these principles can be one of the hardest things to do, so having a loved one who previously agreed with you holding the opposite position can be jarring. But that doesn't necessarily mean that every situation needs to be handled with kid gloves; it simply means that one must consider the amount of indoctrination that has often occurred in a given individual.

Even if you aren't intending to persuade people to give up their religions, even if you couldn't care less what other people believe, when you say, "I don't believe in god(s)," it will always mean that, if they do, you believe they are wrong. This fact is one aspect that separates religious identification with other disagreements and discussions common within families. And it is about a topic that some people hold closer than all else: faith. In fact, that is one of the distinguishing features that separates coming out as an atheist and coming out in the traditional sense as within the LGBTQ community. It is not as if saying, "I'm gay," inherently means, "Straight people are wrong to be straight."

That's part of why coming out as an atheist is so confrontational and one of the main reasons that many people who disbelieve choose to simply remain silent about the issue. Unfortunately, taking that route doesn't progress tolerance toward a secular mindset or educate the believer about secularism, nor does it make it easier for future atheists to be open about their beliefs without fear of reprisal. In fact, an atheist who remains completely silent and/or complies with religious norms out of cultural familiarity (and not due to concerns about safety) may actually make coming out more difficult for others by playing into the assumption that everyone is a theist and increasingly separating people of no religion from the public view.

If there is a familial confrontation as a result of your coming out, it is important to recognize that if your position is by definition opposed to theirs, then the opposite is also true. Just because their position may be more popular (in most regions of the world, including and especially the United States), it does not make it any more reasonable or obvious—in fact, it is quite the opposite. After all, as I discussed earlier, without cultural indoctrination, all of us would be atheists or, more specifically, while many may dream up their own gods as did our ancestors, they would certainly not be "Christian" or "Jewish" or "Muslim" or any other established religion. That's because, without the texts and churches and familial instruction, there are no independent evidences that any specific religion is true. Outside of the Bible, how would one hear of Jesus? Without the Qur'an, how would one know about Muhammad? The same goes for every established religion.

Misunderstandings about atheism also contribute to the "controversial" aspects of coming out. It is not uncommon that a religious person sees your disbelief in their particular Creator as an affront to said Creator. I can't count the number of times I've been accused of "hating God" for simply not believing in any deities—a rather contradictory concept if you think about it. But that does not stop some people from taking another person's atheism as a personal attack on their ideas and their God. This type of cultural stigma is common and can generally be counteracted by education on the basics, starting with the definition of atheist as I discussed earlier: a lack of a belief in a god or gods.

As an "out" and vocal atheist, I've gotten used to hearing religious objections that result from conflicts between believers and nonbelievers . . . one of the most common from Christians is the claim that "Jesus still loves you." While there are often good intentions behind this phrase, for a nonbeliever, it doesn't provide the comfort that it may for a Christian. I, for one, honestly care more about the love here on earth than the possibility of being "loved" by an unprovable and unknowable being. I'm more concerned with the love I share with my family and close friends; it is love that doesn't come with the price of blind faith, and rejection of their love doesn't result in eternal damnation.

"I'll pray for you" is another popular phrase uttered by religious people in interactions with nonbelievers. While some no doubt have positive intentions, this is usually seen as a condescending and self-righteous remark. More often than not, I hear this phrase used by people who have zero intent to go home and literally use their alleged hotline to God to try to save my soul. And saying I'll pray for you to an atheist in this negative manner is like giving the middle finger to a blind person who has upset you. You may feel better, but your empty gesture will go unnoticed. If a believer really thinks their god will alter its divine plan to satisfy his or her requests, though, I like to suggest that they focus all of those prayers on the sick and the dying, and leave me out of them.

Confrontation is a natural part of the coming out experience and of many interactions. And dealing with confrontation is something that people get used to in the context of a family. It may help, however, to make it known that you aren't seeking to change the way they think, but instead that you should have the same freedom of and from religion that most modern governments guarantee their citizens. The fact that, as an open atheist, you are telling believers they're wrong does not necessarily mean that it is a bad thing. In a modern context, being able to voice your opinions and challenge those of the majority is absolutely critical. It is these challenges from nonreligious people all over the world that cause believers to give a second thought to the archaic traditions that they identify with and, in many cases, also ignore. If a situation arises in which the conflict is out of control, it is always best to seek professional guidance in the form of therapy and/or counseling. In chapter 12, "Extreme Situations," you'll find information about how to find secular therapists.

8

BE PREPARED

Before anything else, preparation is the key to success.

—ALEXANDER GRAHAM BELL,
SCOTTISH-BORN INVENTOR

To "hope for the best and prepare for the worst" is helpful advice when approaching such a divisive topic; after all, you don't know how your loved ones will re-act—so be prepared for some unwelcome responses. With the negative connotations that the religious ma-jority has historically bestowed upon secularists and nonreligious individuals (ideas that, unfortunately, continue to be taught in modern churches), there could be a knee-jerk reaction on behalf of your loved ones to respond negatively toward your lack of belief. In Christianity, this can be traced back to hateful scripture such as 2 John 1:9–11: "Anyone who runs ahead and does not continue in the teaching of Christ does not have God; whoever continues in the teaching has both the Father and the Son. If anyone comes to you and does not bring this teaching, do not take them into your house or welcome them. Anyone who welcomes them shares in their wicked work." Other passages, such as 2 Chronicles 15:12–13, actually condone putting atheists to death for their beliefs.* Some of the more closed-minded and fundamentalist believers may even associate your secularism with devil worship or "Satanism." I should not have to point out the ridiculousness of this connection.

Part of the planning process of making your skepticism public knowledge might involve ensuring that you have prepared rational arguments that respond to what issues your family and closest friends may or may not bring up during this interaction or, likelier, series of interactions. For those "active atheists" or atheist activists who generally believe that religion is a negative force in the modern landscape, it is considered common practice to engage in all-out rational debate regarding the existence of god(s) in anonymous interactions with the religious; in this particular case, however, it may be easier to begin by simply adopting a "to each their

---

* 2 Chronicles 15:12–13: "They entered into a covenant to seek the Lord, the God of their ancestors, with all their heart and soul. All who would not seek the Lord, the God of Israel, were to be put to death, whether small or great, man or woman."

own" mentality in which you lovingly accept each other's dogmatic preferences unconditionally. This is not to say, however, that you should not provide reasons for your de-conversion; it simply means that, early on, the best approach may be mildly describing why you have chosen reason over faith. Over time, it is even possible that you might convince your loved ones that they don't need religious doctrines to live happy and full lives, perhaps freeing them from centuries-old supernatural dogmas, too.

Preparation for coming out as an atheist includes choosing wisely how and with whom you begin the process of public de-conversion. Some relatives and loved ones might be more understanding than others; it is advisable to seek these people out for starters. You may want to "test the waters" in this regard by casually bringing up the topic of God and/or religion to those people closest to you whose religious preferences are unknown to you or perhaps those who you imagine might be sympathetic to your cause. It is not the case that all believers will condemn you; there are many open-minded believers who will not see your atheism as inherently bad or offensive. Sometimes, you will be surprised to find out that people you have known your entire life and assumed to be religious are, in fact, skeptics or unconcerned with "divine" matters altogether; this can be a welcoming initial interaction for those who might be scared of judgmental reactions and stressed personal relationships with fundamentalists in the family. There is only one way to find out if some of your loved ones feel the same way as you do. That's not to mention the fact that you could possibly be providing them with the support they need, too.

Just as religion is (ideally) considered to be a personal matter,* it might help to pose your secularism as a similar entity to any fundamentalist family members from whom you fear negative reactions or rejection. In other words, you may want to disclose your atheism in a way that warrants little to no discussion, in order to avoid further interrogations or "sermons." An example of this could be, "I don't want religion to be my motivation for behaving in a moral manner," "I believe in the goodness of humanity," "I have faith in nature," and so on. These types of vague statements discourage further inquiry while retaining a sense of openness and honesty regarding your beliefs surrounding the presence of deities. Being prepared with these types of remarks may

---

* Matthew 6:1–4: "Be careful not to practice your righteousness in front of others to be seen by them. If you do, you will have no reward from your Father in heaven. So when you give to the needy, do not announce it with trumpets, as the hypocrites do in the synagogues and on the streets, to be honored by others. Truly I tell you, they have received their reward in full. But when you give to the needy, do not let your left hand know what your right hand is doing, so that your giving may be in secret. Then your Father, who sees what is done in secret, will reward you."

aid you in dealing with more closed-minded individuals, who otherwise might seek to reconvert you into their religion. That—I should warn—can be a very tedious and dissatisfying argument for both parties.

How can you really prepare for coming out as an atheist to religious kin? Just like anything else, preparation is aided by practice. We already discussed the option (when available) to contact a less-religious, maybe distant, relative or acquaintance who might be more understanding of your secularism, but what about those of us who do not have the luxury of being acquainted with such an individual? This is where online forums, blogs, and chat rooms become useful. All over the internet there exist websites specifically dedicated to the discussion of religion, atheism, religious tolerance, and rational free thought.

Interaction with other skeptics and believers with whom you aren't acquainted on a personal level will help you to be vocal about your secularism without worrying about consequences in your daily life; it is also important, however, to not carry over any disrespectful or begrudging tones from these anonymous interactions into your conversations with those you love and for whom you care. In those familiar cases, it is often simpler to show as much love and respect as possible in the engagement, if for no other reason than to show that your secularism hasn't affected any sense of "morals" or "proper behavior" that they saw in you in the past, for this is a common misconception among religious people being presented with secularism for the first time in a personal and formal dynamic.

9

COMING OUT TO YOUR SIGNIFICANT OTHER

> We are told that people stay in love because of chemistry, or because they remain intrigued with each other, because of many kindnesses, because of luck. But part of it has got to be forgiveness and gratefulness.
>
> —ELLEN GOODMAN, JOURNALIST

Coming out as a nonbeliever to a fundamentalist or otherwise religious spouse is one of the most difficult situations involving de-conversion. It is easy to see how a marriage or partnership might suffer from such a divisive distinction being revealed between the two partners. But on the other hand, what can be more crucial in such an important relationship than being honest and sincere with one another? Above all else, it is important to remember that this can be a survivable interaction, even if your partner is fervently dedicated to a specific tradition, if it is approached in a manner in which the concerns of both individuals are properly addressed. By introducing your secularism to your spouse or partner in a calm and understanding manner, you can ensure a smooth interaction as long as you make it abundantly clear to your significant other that this newly announced difference in faith will not affect the terms of your established relationship.

The True Love Argument, which addresses love and the Christian concept of "heaven," might help you convey to your partner why the ideas of True Love and the Christian doctrine are truly incompatible. I will excerpt this complex yet concise argument from a prior five-step description of it in my first book, *Disproving Christianity and Other Secular Writings:*

> *Heaven, as described by the Christian tradition, is eternal happiness in communion with God.*
>
> *True love consists of a relationship in which neither party can be genuinely happy without the other.*
>
> *Two people in a relationship of this nature could, because of different beliefs, be separated in the afterlife, and one could be sent to heaven, without his or her significant other.*
>
> *The Christian in heaven could not be happy without his or her partner, thus causing heaven to*

become a place of everlasting pain and sadness: a hell.

Because heaven is described as eternal happiness, this creates a contradiction in which the concept of a Christian heaven fails to be viable.

Therefore Christianity, which presupposes eternal bliss in heaven postmortem, cannot be the true Word of an all-knowing God.

Coming out as a nonbeliever to your spouse or significant other becomes increasingly crucial when the possibility of interaction with children comes into play. Whether you have children already or plan to in the future, the question will inevitably arise regarding how you and your partner will raise the children in terms of religious ideologies. Your partner may want to share the wonders of his or her religious tradition with the child while it is just as likely that you, probably having experienced and rejected this type of religious indoctrination, might hope to prevent this behavior. It may be the case that neither partner can convince the other to change ideological positions on the issue and, in that instance, there are cases in which each parent presents their ideas surrounding religion and spirituality as the time arises, without unity. While this is not ideal, it may be better than compromising what you sincerely believe in order to satisfy your partner's desires to teach children that a specific tradition is "the right one." A healthier compromise in the decision of how to introduce religion to your children (if at all), would be one in which the parents work collaboratively to teach about various religious traditions and scientific positions simultaneously, letting the kids decide for themselves whether or not to adopt a spiritual or naturalistic understanding of the universe. It is important to note that more serious interactions—like the scenario described above—may warrant professional guidance or counseling.

Whether or not children come into play when making the decision to come out as a nonbeliever to your significant other, it is one of the most difficult decisions that you may have to face throughout your journey to becoming a public nonbeliever. The importance of this decision, however, does not translate into the importance of the difference itself: highlighting the similarities in mentality between yourself and your partner, as opposed to the differences, will help him or her in understanding exactly how little religious differences matter in the big picture. Discussing how your moral compass has remained untainted, for example, might assist in shifting the conversation from religious differences to ideological similarities. To further shed light on the topic of religion, atheism, and relationships, I'll excerpt from an interview with Nickolas Johnson, who is an atheist and secular humanist who is married to a Christian:

A year or so later I met another girl. A Christian girl. After a few years of dating, we married in her church (her choice) in July 2007. In the first year of our marriage, I began reading more nonfiction books. I started with Why People Believe Weird Things, *and then was hooked on free thought–style books. A few months after we married, my wife fell and greatly injured her back. The next few years were especially difficult for the two of us. The injury caused her to have two surgeries, and I had to leave my job to stay at home to take care of her. Throughout all of this, I'm sure many people probably would expect some sort of shift in faith from one or both of us, but our opinions remained intact. Her religious faith seemed unscathed, and my atheism only grew more fervent with the more knowledge I gained. I never questioned or blamed God, because it seemed futile, and I think she must have found some sort of peace with her views.*

My wife and I have been married for nearly five years now, and I think religion plays a bigger role in my life than it does in hers. I like to read books regarding biblical historicity and logical arguments while she goes to her old church back where her mother lives whenever she's in the area. Sometimes my opinions of her religion may seem reflective of her, but I'm not brash because of some sort of disdain for that part of her personality; more so I have an open, honest relationship with her and nothing is too taboo to talk about. Her views on religion have always been what I would call "Diet Christian," but I suppose everyone else just refers to as liberal; that has allowed us to discuss things without getting into any irrational arguments. When it all boils down to it, if you share the same core values and put importance in the same values it really isn't that hard to be with someone that disagrees with you on other things. There are certain things she is passionate about that I do not much care for and vice versa, so we never have any reason to argue over those things. There are also certain things, like prayer, that we may not agree on, but it is not something we bother arguing over. She has a very open mind and is going to two free-thought conferences with me this year.

If I had to give any advice to someone who has opposing opinions of a loved one in regard to religion it would be this: stay calm, try to keep an open mind, don't interrupt, and never lose sight of why you're talking with the person in the first place.

10

ESTABLISHING A NEW SENSE OF COMMUNITY

Indeed, organizing atheists has been compared to herding cats, because they tend to think independently and will not conform to authority. But a good first step would be to build up a critical mass of those willing to "come out," thereby encouraging others to do so. Even if they can't be herded, cats in sufficient numbers can make a lot of noise and they cannot be ignored.

—RICHARD DAWKINS, *THE GOD DELUSION*

From weekly church services and gatherings to summer camps and holiday events, a religion often fosters a sense of community for its followers. Many people who transition out of a religion and were previously involved in the social aspects of their religious traditions find this to be one of the most difficult parts about leaving the faith. In these cases, it is not uncommon for a church to have provided most of one's sense of community—and losing that can be a big deal.

In some fundamentalist and rural religious communities, the church provides the vast majority of social interactions in a person's life. An individual might be born into a family in which everything—from education to extracurricular activities—is governed or sponsored by a particular church. In these cases, leaving the religion can be more difficult than simply coming out. Many times, these individuals are forced to give up everything they've ever known if they make the courageous step to leave their religion. This is especially true in certain sects of the Church of Jesus Christ of Latter-day Saints—or Mormon—religion, which is itself a denomination of Christianity founded in the 1820s as a form of Christian primitivism. In these situations, a dramatic relocation is sometimes necessary.

For those whose entire lives may not revolve around religion—but that a new sense of community would be helpful after losing the church community—there are quite a few options. For starters, some sites like Meetup (www.meetup.com) provide a platform for groups to schedule and organize secular events. Like religious organizations, some of these groups plan weekly gatherings and/or discussion groups—but they aren't limited to atheist topics. Some meetings are centered on a holiday, and others simply provide an event for nontheists to attend with like-minded people—examples include barbecues, book clubs, pool parties, and so on.

Having like-minded friends and social acquaintances is important, especially when a nonbeliever's current friends and family are not supportive of his or her religious stance. As is the case in all instances of discrimination or social tension, talking and sharing ideas with people who face similar issues is a helpful therapeutic tool. Talking openly about your nonbelief with nonjudgmental people you already know is obviously ideal, but for many, that's not an option.

If you, as is the case with many who make the transition out of a religion, feel as though it takes away from your practiced holiday celebrations, there are plenty of nonreligious options for annual traditions, too. Websites like Secular Seasons (www.secularseasons.org) list humanist celebrations and events focused on the separation of church and state, free thought, and rational thought. Others, like me, choose to celebrate the common holiday traditions and simply separate the religious component.

For many, developing a new sense of community takes place online. There are thousands of secular websites and groups on larger platforms dedicated to atheist dating and networking, and can provide a safe haven for discussion about separation of church and state, religious criticisms, and other secular issues. There are also numerous groups, pages, and communities on Facebook—as well as other major social networks.

For children, "church camps" are all too common. These camps provide children opportunities to socialize and learn important skills but are also extremely useful tools for indoctrination. Many camps have some sort of religious agenda, but there are options for those of us who don't wish to send our children to a camp where they might be told what to believe. Camp Quest, an Ohio-based "summer camp beyond belief," provides an educational adventure shaped by fun, friends, free thought, science, and humanist values. They also provide virtual options.* The camp offers a mix of traditional summer camp activities and educational activities related to the Camp Quest mission. If you're an atheist parent, you should also note the website Atheist Parents (www.atheistparents.org), which hosts parenting resources, including articles, forums, a blog, and related links.

For those secularists who miss the larger church gatherings, there are numerous conventions, conferences, and rallies that are dedicated to sharing the message of free thought and skepticism. Here are just a few:

- American Humanist Association Annual Conference: The American Humanist Association (AHA) is an educational organization in the United States that advances humanism, a pro-

---

* http://www.campquest.org.

gressive philosophy of life that, without theism or other supernatural beliefs, affirms the ability and responsibility of human beings to lead personal lives of ethical fulfillment that aspire to the greater good of humanity. AHA was founded in 1941 and currently provides legal assistance to defend the constitutional rights of secular and religious minorities, actively lobbies Congress on church-state separation and progressive issues, and maintains a grassroots network of 150 local affiliates and chapters that engage in social activism, philosophical discussion, and community-building events.

- Committee for Skeptical Inquiry Convention (CSICon): CSICon is dedicated to scientific inquiry and critical thinking. The conference is produced by the Committee for Skeptical Inquiry in collaboration with *Skeptical Inquirer* magazine and the Center for Inquiry.

- Freedom from Religion Foundation Annual National Convention: The Freedom from Religion Foundation (FFRF) promotes the constitutional principle of separation of state and church and educates the public on matters relating to nontheism. Incorporated in 1978 in Wisconsin, the foundation is a national membership association of more than seventeen thousand freethinkers, atheists, agnostics, and skeptics of any pedigree.

The foundation is a nonprofit, tax-exempt, educational organization under Internal Revenue Code 501(c)(3). All dues and contributions are deductible for income tax purposes.*

- Global Atheist Convention: The Global Atheist Convention is an annual secular gathering based in Melbourne, Australia. The event is sponsored by the Atheist Foundation of Australia Inc., which began in South Australia in 1970 when the members of the Rationalist Association of South Australia decided that a name change would proclaim their basic philosophy, which began in Greece 2,500 years ago.**

- Reason Rally: The Reason Rally is a movement-wide event sponsored by the country's major secular organizations. The intent is to unify, energize, and embolden secular people nationwide, while dispelling the negative opinions held by so much of American society.***

- Skepticon: Skepticon is an annual skeptics convention set in Springfield, Missouri. Springfield is home to the Assemblies of God and several religious universities (such as Evangel and Drury). The area is affectionately referred to by many lo-

---

* http://www.ffrf.org/outreach/convention.
** http://www.atheistconvention.org.au.
*** http://www.reasonrally.org.

cals as the buckle of the Bible Belt. In the fall of 2008, JT Eberhard, Lauren Lane, and the MSU chapter of the Church of the Flying Spaghetti Monster invited P. Z. Myers and Richard Carrier to the Missouri State campus to criticize belief in god. The event was well-attended and was retroactively dubbed Skepticon.*

This is only a small sampling of some of the larger atheist/agnostic conferences and conventions. There are a growing number of similar events each year and, depending on your area, there may be numerous local events, too.

In addition to the various educational events and conferences listed above and the internet groups mentioned earlier, there are many localized organizations dedicated to secularism and/or humanism. There are comprehensive lists of such meeting groups at www.atheists.meetup.com and www.infidels.org/org/local.html; other websites also serve as great resources for identifying these local groups. If you are a student or interested in affiliating yourself with secular groups on college or high school campuses, the Secular Student Alliance has compiled a list of resources available here: https://secularstudents.org/resources-for-students/.

---

* http://www.skepticon.org.

11

I'M ACTUALLY AN ATHEIST

I'm an atheist, and that's it. I believe there's
nothing we can know except that we should
be kind to each other and do what we can for
people.

—KATHARINE HEPBURN,
AMERICAN ACTRESS

This story has it all: tornadoes, cute cats, and a live
CNN interview that went viral, changing the course of
one woman's life.

There is unlikely to be a more public example of an
atheist coming-out story than that of Rebecca Vitsmun,
who was a closeted atheist for about ten years before she
was outed through a spur-of-the-moment comment no
one could have anticipated. She was already open with
fellow atheists that she met online, but almost no one
else knew her true feelings about faith, including her
mother, who was herself devoutly religious.

Then one day in 2013, the unpredictable happened: a class EF5 tornado barreled toward Rebecca's home in Oklahoma. She and her young son escaped just in time, but when they came home, there was little left to recognize. In the wake of the disaster, people looked for an uplifting story and found Rebecca, who changed everything with the simple sentence, "I'm actually an atheist."

Rebecca grew up in a household dominated by religion, with her mother's family being Spanish Catholic and her father's being firm Southern Baptists. She had what she describes as her first "I don't know if that's right" moment when she was fourteen years old and reciting the Nicene Creed as part of her church services. It reads, in part: "We believe in one, holy, Catholic, and apostolic Church."

"I remember thinking I don't think Baptists are going to hell, and I don't think Methodists are going to hell," Rebecca told me in a video interview.

As many future atheists do, fourteen-year-old Rebecca pushed those doubts back to the deepest parts of her mind to preserve her worldview based on inherited dogma. So much so that, at seventeen years old, she was voted most likely to become a nun later in life. But repressing questions about faith never works out for long, and she became an atheist at just nineteen years old.

"My mom always said as soon as I was confirmed I could do what I want, so I did that to get my Spanish-

Catholicism mom back pat," she said, referencing a sacred Catholic tradition. "I continued on that path until I got confirmed, and then I started to question everything."

You might think those questions marked the end of Rebecca's journey into atheism, but it was really just the beginning. Despite being a nineteen-year-old atheist, she didn't know there were other nonbelievers out there, too.

"I was just walking around alone. It was in college . . . I was a math major, and I was very frustrated," she said. "I was finding solutions to problems I didn't have, and I was basing my entire life structure on something that didn't make sense to me anymore."

To try to make sense of things in her life, and perhaps to find out which belief system is the right one, Rebecca decided to switch her emphasis in school to comparative religions. It was through the course of her studies on faith that she realized the truth: all religions serve as a middleman to get people thinking about morality.

After graduating from college with a degree in something she didn't truly believe in, Rebecca moved to New Jersey, and then to New York, and then to Oklahoma. She was an atheist, but almost no one in her personal life knew about that. She had to hide that part of herself because of her family, who were mostly religious people with good intentions, and because of the extremely faith-based community in which she and her family were living.

And then the tornado hit. Cowering in her bathtub with her nineteen-month-old son, Anders, Rebecca made a last-minute decision to take her son and run for their lives. She started driving, only to remember that she had left her two cats at the doomed house.

When she returned to check on her house and look for her cats, she was met with a bittersweet surprise. The house had been destroyed, standing just at her knees, but the cats had survived. Since the whole family had escaped major injuries, it was actually a pretty uplifting story. So, she uploaded a photo to her CNN iReport account.

Enter Wolf Blitzer, a major news icon working for CNN. His team emailed Rebecca for an interview, and she obliged, bringing along her young son. The discussion was pretty ordinary until the end, when Wolf Blitzer looked for a way to close the positive segment. He turned to Anders, who had been repeating things he heard from the adults, and said, "Say, 'I'm Anders, and this is CNN.'"

"Anders gives him nothing. Just dead air on live television," Rebecca said. "They have to think on their feet and come up with something immediately, so that's when he asked me about the Lord."

That's when it happened, the exchange heard around the world. Wolf Blitzer asked this woman who had just survived a tornado whether she thanked the Lord. In Oklahoma, it'd probably be a safe bet that she'd say yes. But Wolf Blitzer lost that bet on live national television.

"You're blessed. Brian, your husband, is blessed. Anders is blessed. We're happy you're here; you guys did a great job," Blitzer said in a slightly awkward moment. "I guess you've got to thank the Lord, right? Do you thank the Lord for that split-second decision?"

In that moment, Rebecca said she was thinking one thing and one thing only: "I can't lie." But a simple *no* wouldn't have been satisfactory, so she blurted out what popped into her head next.

"I . . . I . . . I'm actually an atheist, but I don't blame anybody for thanking the Lord," Rebecca said, laughing.

That moment of Rebecca coming out atheist has been the subject of news reports, interviews, and podcasts and has been featured in books and videos. It even led comedian Doug Stanhope to crowdfund $126,000 to help her. It changed Rebecca's life and has helped her change others'.

In 2020, I sat down to talk with Rebecca about her experiences following the viral moment and what she has learned in the last seven years.

MCAFEE: OK, so take me back to when you said, "I'm actually an atheist," to Wolf Blitzer live on CNN. Did it feel good to tell the truth in that moment, despite there being potential consequences with family and friends?

VITSMUN: At that moment, there was nothing other than answering the question on my mind. I did know the consequences were coming, I guess, but I did not consider fallout. I only considered the fact that I need to not lie. I don't do that. I would just pour truth out of my face before a lie comes out . . . I'm a verbal-diarrhea, get-myself-in-trouble level, not a liar. I'll confess stuff if I feel like it's on my conscience at all. I don't even like holding on to birthday presents because it feels like a lie. It's sort of like I'm just walking around keeping secrets, and that makes me feel uncomfortable. So, I knew I wasn't going to lie, but he asked if I thank the Lord. I can't just say, "No." That's so awkward! So, what's the truth? Why am I saying no to this question? That's super weird. And then I was like, "I'm actually an atheist." And then I laughed.

MCAFEE: When did you start thinking there might be some repercussions from all your honesty?

VITSMUN: After the interview, I started to think something could be wrong. I was thinking, "Who was even watching that? I'm pretty sure my husband's grandparents were watching that . . ." So, I called my husband, and I'm like, "Hey, the interview went great, but there was this part at the end where it was weird, and he asked me if I thank the Lord." And he was like, "Oh my god, what did you say?" because he knew right away that I'm just verbal diarrhea, and I told him I said I was an atheist. And he goes, "You said what?! My grandparents were watching that!" And I'm like, "Yeah, I know, maybe you should tell your dad before he finds out from them," because he wasn't out, either! Then I get home and I have hundreds of friend requests, I've been tagged in like fifty videos, and it is spreading like wildfire.

MCAFEE: It's interesting that you immediately laughed and then added the caveat that you don't blame anyone else for thanking God. Why did you feel that was important to mention?

VITSMUN: I once watched a thing that said why people laugh is because something unexpected happens. And I just said I was an atheist on live television, and I had been hiding that forever, and here I am just . . . blah. It's one of the funniest moments in my life! It's so absurd. Actual absurdity. Then I was proud of myself for getting out my next sentence, which was that I don't blame anybody for thanking the Lord. I didn't want anyone out there to think that the word *atheist* meant I wasn't appreciative of the sentiment. It's like, I'm not thanking the Lord, but please thank your Lord for my survival. Yeah! Use whatever language you want to say, "Yay, a mommy and a baby survived." I don't ever say

I'm an atheist without also saying I don't give a shit. It's like, I'm an atheist, but it's fine if you're whatever.

MCAFEE: One of the first things you did when you and your baby survived the tornado was text your mom, who replied, "Praise Jesus!" So, technically, she brought up this issue of thanking the Lord before Blitzer. How did she and the rest of your family react to the interview and to the fact that you were actually an atheist?

VITSMUN: My mom told me I wasn't really an atheist. I was like, "Yeah, I am," and at first, she was like, "No, you're not, because you believe in a higher power." And I was like, "I don't believe in a higher power, Mom. I wouldn't have said the word *atheist* unless I knew what it meant." And my dad was just disappointed.

But my mom had already been conditioned on some level on how to love me because of when I came out to her as polyamorous in 2006. My parents knew I was poly way before they knew I was an atheist, and I was an atheist way before I was poly. But they learned how to love me as poly. My mom would call, and then she'd say something rude, and then I'd be like, "Hey, here's your one warning of the day, and if you say anything again, I'm going to hang up and you can try again tomorrow." And then she'd say something again, and I'd be like, "OK, better luck tomorrow!" And so, she got to the point where I wasn't hanging up on her anymore.

So, I was very proud of my mom. I was like, "Damn, you've learned how to love me. That's so kind. Yay!" It felt really good.

Because of that past experience, I didn't have to spend the time hanging up on her, which would have been my strategy, truly. Which is like, if you say something, I'm going to give you a warning, and then if you do it again, you can call back the next day. And I'll answer. And then if you do it again, I'll hang up again, and we can try again the next day. And I'll keep that going eternally until we learn how to communicate. But I don't want to cut them off. I want to give them opportunities. I want to give them as many opportunities as it takes.

It was a big deal in communicating with my mom about something she didn't like about me to continuously give her more chances, just permanently on some level just being okay with hanging up on my mom forever, unless she learns something, which she did. It took some months, but she did. So, for this, she was like, "Well, even if you are an atheist, I know you're a good person." And I was like, "Thank you!"

But the thing is, my mom and dad aren't the only family members I have, so I have every single family member, which is Spanish Catholic on one side and Southern Baptist on the other. And so, the Spanish ones were like, "Don't tell Grandma." Everyone was fine. Some of them have been institutionalized. Nobody is judging anybody over there. That's another reason my mom is primed for acceptance.

But my dad's side, there's a lawyer, an Olympic diver, and a ballerina. We owned a golf course. Me, my dad, my family, owned one. So it's super different on that side. Way more judgmental. My grandmother will wait by the trash cans for the trash man to show up so she can talk to them about Jesus. She's the kind of lady that tells my mom she can't read Harry Potter because it's of the devil, *700 Club* is always on over there, that kind of stuff. So, they were like, "Never let Mimi know. Never let Mimi know." She's still that Southern Baptist speaker, and her grandchild is an atheist.

So, everybody in both families was just hiding it from the grandmas. That was essentially the overtone of everything: permanently hide it from the grandmothers. But I'd have them also tell me things like, "I'm praying for you," and I was like, "Well, I think positive thoughts about you, as well." I just found sentences to say that were positive because I'm not interested in being upset with them. There's also some level of, I'm comfortable with me, and if they're not, that's a "them" thing. If they want to say something is wrong with me, then I would say, "OK, well, only one of us has a problem."

MCAFEE: We all know about how you came out to the world as an atheist, but who did you confide in before that? How did that go?

VITSMUN: I was twenty-five, and I moved from New York to Oklahoma with my brother. So, I was in Oklahoma, and I met people and became a part of the society there. I found out through meetup.com that they had an atheist group, and I was like, "What? OK." So, I went to this atheist group, and they were just like a once-a-month meetup-at-a-pizza-place kind of group. And I was like, "OK, I can go eat pizza with these atheists sometimes and talk to people who think like me. Holy crap! This is amazing!" It was my first time being around people like me. And one of these times, I met this guy, and it was his first time, and I sat across from him, and his name was Red McCall, and he ended up being the president of Oklahoma Atheists later and was the one who completely transformed it from a once-a-month pizza thing to, they have things going on all over. Oklahoma City is one of the biggest cities by land, and so now they have stuff going on all over town, like tennis and business lunches and this and that! They have stuff going on all the time. It became huge under him, which is funny because he's one of the first atheists I ever met.

Red posted on my Facebook after we met, "It was nice meeting you, heathen." And I messaged him like, "I am not out. People don't know I'm an atheist. This is not a thing. Please remove your comment." I was like, not cool, man! Because my parents didn't know, my co-workers didn't know, my friends who weren't in that group didn't know, and I wasn't about to tell them. Not even close. And I would answer questions honestly, but nobody ever just said, "Are you an atheist?" or like, "Do you thank the Lord?" like Wolf Blitzer. Nobody ever pushed it. I would have said it had they pushed it, but I wasn't offering that information at all.

MCAFEE: When you came out as an atheist on CNN, did you get any shocking reactions? Being on live TV, I imagine you could have received death threats.

VITSMUN: I didn't read the comment sections because I started off reading and it was really quick that I got to one that said my baby should have died to teach me a lesson, and I'm like, "What kind of sicko wishes death on a baby?! And they think they're religious!" So, I just cried, and I was permanently done with comment sections about myself. I'm sure there were death threats. I was told that there were, but I didn't care. They were wishing death on my nineteen-month-old baby, so I'm not having anything to do with that.

MCAFEE: What about positive interactions throughout the coming-out process?

VITSMUN: My husband's brother-in-law came out before me. He was raised Mormon and was on a mission in Brazil. He was starting to lose his religion down there, and he was trying to convince them to let him leave, but they wouldn't let him leave. Instead, they were going to drug him, they were going to put him on medication and keep him down there and force him to continue his mission. They said depression is normal, and we're going to give you this medication. So, he started taking it and continuing his Mormon mission, which made it much worse, because essentially these people were drugging him and forcing him to continue. Gross! He was super traumatized by that.

So, he came back and sent a message to the whole family, saying, "I'm an apostate." He called himself an apostate. Then we said, "Come over here, we're atheists, too." But we didn't tell anyone else that. We told him we'd take him in, and he could use our extra room. He went to BYU, so he was at BYU, in Utah, surrounded by Mormons, and his family is full of Mormons, and everyone he knows is Mormon. He had nobody else in the world but us. He stayed with us, and he got into school, and he got accepted into a program later and moved off, and now he's an atheist pharmacist. We didn't expect that! After we took him in, people thought badly of us for taking in the apostate. And then they found out later that we were atheists! Even him coming forward wasn't enough for us to say, "Well, us, too."

MCAFEE: My guess is that, even someone like you, who went through the most public atheist outing of all time, still has to tell certain people that you're an atheist from time to time. Would you agree that coming out atheist is more of a continual process than a simple, onetime event?

VITSMUN: I come out atheist all the time. I come out atheist constantly, nonstop, any time that it's even sort of even remotely alluded to. I just say it now. I love saying it. I appreciate saying it. There haven't been circumstances where I regretted it.

When it comes to the "onetime thing," yeah, that sort of handled a lot of people real fast. Everyone I knew at the time found out. But I meet new people constantly. I have doctors. I have therapists. I moved to Washington, so I have these neighbors. The thing is, at first, I wasn't somebody who was used to saying it. But I was getting messages from people saying, "Hey, I thought about you today because this circumstance came up for me to say it, and I said it!" And I'm like, "Yay, I'm inspiring people to talk about being an atheist all the time!" But why am I not inspiring myself? Why am I still not saying it? Why am I walking around like I have any business not saying it anymore? So, I just started doing it, and then I decided that it was actually really awesome.

And then I started wearing T-shirts and flying to Southern states. I love wearing atheist shirts in Southern states. It's so fun because there's two reactions you'll get if you're wearing an atheist T-shirt in a Southern state. And one is they do not want to be near you, and they go away. Nice. Or they come running toward you and are your new best friend! How many amazing people have I met by wearing an atheist T-shirt? They are like, "Oh my god, I'm an atheist, too! I've never met another atheist." I've had emotional people come up to me like, "You're so brave!" And I'm like, if you wear one, people like you come up and everyone else just turns around and goes somewhere else. I'm just letting you know: if you want to find your people, just go wear an atheist shirt, and I guarantee you, I've never fought a battle over it.

MCAFEE: Do you think more people coming out as atheists could help other closeted nonbelievers who also hope to go public one day, perhaps by showing the believing majority that anyone can be an atheist and it doesn't change who they really are?

VITSMUN: Absolutely. I have so many friends who are not atheists who know I'm an atheist and use me as an example for when they realize that atheists aren't bad people. They're like, "Before you, I had this picture of an atheist in my mind, and it was like somebody who was bleeding goats or something, and you're just this nice mom and you're just a person." They say they don't agree with me but that I'm not mean and I don't feel the need to change them. And I'm like, "Exactly." I would never go to a religious person and be like, "Come to the dark side," or something like that. If they asked me or had any questions, I'd answer them honestly, but I'm not going to go be pushy about my thoughts, because I don't want anybody to come be pushy about their thoughts at me, either. But I have a lot of friends now who have lots of backgrounds, and they're all fine with me being an atheist, and I'm fine with them being whatever they are. Of course, I've also had the kind that were fine with me being an atheist, and they were fine with their religion, until they were no longer fine with their religion and they became atheists and came to me. That's happened, too, of course, over the course of time.

MCAFEE: What are some of the false and negative atheist stereotypes you encountered from believers while in Oklahoma?

VITSMUN: One time, I walked into the lunchroom, and the conversation at the lunch table was about how atheists are really Satanists that worship the devil. And my contribution was not to say I was an atheist. Instead, I said, "Well, I thought they didn't believe in the devil, either." And then they laughed! They're like, "Oh, you're so naive, Rebecca!" And I thought, "How would I know? I guess I'm just this naive person who isn't aware of all this knowledge you guys have." These are just my coworkers. What happens if they think I'm a devil worshipper? I got to find out what happens if they think that you're a devil worshipper . . . One of the women wouldn't come near me after I went viral. She stayed far away and had this look on her face like, "Don't come near me." But I didn't work there anymore. I was a stay-at-home mom, but three of the women were just like, "Oh, I didn't know that about you." I thought I would have lost everybody, and that was not the case. I think I lost one. I just thought that the conversation at the table that day was led by everybody, but in retrospect, maybe it was one person pushing the conversation and everybody was able to contribute on some level . . . maybe everybody else was just playing along with how much they cared. Now I look back and I see these people who I was afraid of and afraid of their reactions, and how many have reacted poorly? A small number. Very small. People actually cared who I was, and they didn't forget who I was. The ones who did were their own thing, and I could easily be like, well, that's a "them" thing.

MCAFEE: You know better than most what it's like to come out as an atheist in a major way. What would you tell closeted atheists who might come from circumstances similar to yours? What would you tell Rebecca before that tornado in Oklahoma?

VITSMUN: I would definitely start with, "Just do it," although there's more to that. I've spent a lot of time on healing and developing tools for how to recover from scenarios, and what I've been able to come up with is a system of five different points that I think are the most important to focus on in life. This is my life system.

The first one is safety. Safety first, obviously. So, if you're in danger of physical harm, safety first . . . but get out of there! If you're in danger of physical harm, start a plan to get out of the scenario as fast as possible.

And then step two is identity. Yourself. You. Everything that's you. Just start being you. You, you, you, you. If you're an atheist, be you; if you're gay, be you; if you think you don't understand your identity or what gender you are or gender at all, and you know nothing, just say, "Hey, I actually know nothing!" Whatever it is that's in there, just start proclaiming that, as soon as you're safe. Safety first, and then out with it and see what happens from there. Because if you're not being your identity, you're not going to be able to form any kind of autonomous connection with anybody because you're kind of going in with a lie. So, safety first, obviously, but as soon as your home is safe, just go! If you lose all your friends, they were shitty friends. You won't lose all your friends, though. You won't. There are going to be people who immediately want to see past that because they love you so much. They're just not going to care, because they don't want to lose you. You matter too much to their life. They've put in so many hours and they'll just think, "Oh no, you've been walking around with that inside of you for all this time. That must have been painful." You can tell them you were scared, too. You can tell them all these things that were keeping you from sharing your identity so you can move past that point.

Next is autonomy and connection. They're separate things, but they kind of come at the same time. It's like me, me, you, you. Separate, but connected. But to be able to have an autonomous connection, you have to have a firm sense of your identity and be able to share it.

The fifth one is growth. You work on yourself, you find little parts of yourself that need help, and you find all the tools and you focus on that. You build your life around what your needs are, and then you see about the needs of those around you. Then you can grow from there.

So, if anybody is struggling with it, step one, safety, and step two, identity. Get safe and be you. Don't even talk to people and try to get close to them if you can't be you! "You" so hard and then you'll be very happy with what comes from that because you'll be able to have that kind of close, meaningful connection that all human beings on the planet are seeking.

MCAFEE: Having been a closeted atheist in a religious family, what would you say to families of those who are coming out? For instance, what would you tell a Christian mom who just found out her kid is an atheist?

VITSMUN: Well, first I would say, "Calm down, it's going to be OK." Then I'd tell them to slowly ask questions and listen. You don't have to change who you are to accept somebody who is different. Their beliefs, or nonbeliefs, are not attacks. Just because they think differently, that doesn't mean they need help. They don't need to change. They need acceptance where they're at and where they're telling you they're at. Start by telling them that you love them, and that this won't change that, and then I'd honestly suggest just starting with talking, slowly. Having small conversations and be respectful. If you guys ever get into something that's hard, space. No one needs to go into an interaction that's hard, ever. If it starts getting to be a little too much, back up, calm down, try again. Then back up, calm down, try again. Until at some point, you can be together and understand that this person believes and this person doesn't, and that's OK.

Fighting with family is hard. I've fought so many fights with my family. My dad was a Fox News–watching, Tea Party dude who loved Glenn Beck and would quote him, so fighting is real.

MCAFEE: It has been several years since your public outing, and your family has had some time to get over their initial reactions. Where do they stand now?

VITSMUN: My mom, up until a couple of years ago, would still send me a text every now and then that was like, "God gave me a daughter" kind of stuff, and I used to send her back like, "I'm still an atheist!" For a little while, she'd be like, "Have you tried going to church?"

She did try for a little bit. And I'd be like, "Please stop asking me," and she did stop asking. At this point, they don't talk about it anymore. It's sort of like living up here in Washington, where it's like, that's just an accepted thing. No need to discuss it. We don't need to sit here and discuss it because there's nothing to figure out. They don't need to talk about it, and I don't need to talk about it. Here we are standing side by side and we're talking about food and the kids and what I want to do next month and what their plans are, just what our lives are like. My mom might be like, "Oh, I'm going to church, and I need to get ready," but she's not trying to use that. It's not passive-aggressive jabby. That's just her life.

MCAFEE: When I first decided to write this book, it was because I was rejected from a graduate program for being an "atheist activist with an axe to grind." Have you ever had the atheist issue come up in a work environment or some other more professional setting? Have you ever experienced discrimination for your lack of outward religious faith?

VITSMUN: When it came to professional settings since I've come out, I haven't had a job that paid me outside of atheism, which is cool because I finally used my degree. I got a degree in atheism, and I totally used it! I have volunteered a lot, and I'm an open atheist when I volunteer. I say it, usually. If anybody broaches a religious conversation, I'll say, "I'm an atheist, but I'm OK with everybody's religion." But it hasn't affected much because I caveat that fast. Even when I went viral, I caveated that by saying that I'm OK with everybody's religion. But it hasn't affected much because I caveat that fast.

Rebecca bravely proclaimed to the world that she was an atheist on live TV, shocking her entire family and many of her religious friends. But, as we will tell you, that wouldn't be the last time she would come out about her lack of faith. Now, she counts herself lucky to say she's an atheist and encourages others to do the same.

While Rebecca may have lost a few people who she once considered friends, she also found something bigger: a community of like-minded thinkers. I think her story perfectly encapsulates what it means to come out atheist.

---— 12 ——

EXTREME SITUATIONS

> In extreme situations, the entire universe
> becomes our foe; at such critical times, unity of
> mind and technique is essential—do not let
> your heart waver!
>
> —MORIHEI UESHIBA,
> JAPANESE MARTIAL ARTIST

In some regions, being an atheist—or even professing a religion different from those that the government sanctions—is not only a crime but a crime that is punishable by death. And, contrary to popular belief, blasphemy laws still exist in some parts of the world, and they are often strictly enforced. There are very few instances in which remaining silent about your non-belief is a good idea—but there are exceptions to every rule.

In February 2012, an atheist in Indonesia was jailed for nothing more than a comment on Facebook in which he said he did not believe in God, according to Al Jazeera, an independent broadcaster owned by the state of Qatar.*

Although Indonesia is officially a "secular" nation, every citizen has to have a religion and register himself according to one of the official five religions—as recognized by the government.

This instance is just one of many across the globe and especially in highly religious areas in the Middle East, speaking out against the state religion is considered blasphemy, and it is not uncommon to see the death penalty imposed for such actions. In the United Kingdom, the death penalty for blasphemy was abolished in 1676, but blasphemy was still a crime in England and Wales until March 2008.

In Iran and some other constitutional Islamic theocracies, the law against blasphemy is derived from Sharia, the moral code and religious law of Islam. Blasphemers are usually charged with "spreading corruption on earth," or mofsed-e-filarz, which can also be applied to political crimes. The law against blasphemy complements laws against criticizing the Islamic regime,

---

* Ileanna Llorens, "Indonesian Atheist Attacked, Faces Jail Time After Posting 'God Doesn't Exist' on Facebook," *HuffPost*, January 20, 2012, http://www.huffingtonpost.com/2012/01/20/atheist-attacked-faces-jail-time-facebook-god_n_1219778.html.

insulting Islam, and publishing materials that deviate from Islamic standards.*

These laws are commonplace in fundamentally Islamic nations—in fact, in May 2012, Kuwait's parliament approved a law that calls for the death penalty for insulting the Muslim prophet Muhammad or his wives and relatives. In an era in which you'd expect scientific progress to impede the emergence of violent religious fundamentalism, it is sad to see that, in some areas of the world, the tide is turning in the opposite direction.

My point in describing these violent and discriminatory acts against atheists around the world is not to dissuade anyone from being open about their lack of supernatural belief—instead, it is to illuminate the negative force of many religions against nonbelievers, even in modern times. If you feel that your life will be endangered by being vocal about your atheism, I would certainly not recommend doing so—but, perhaps, it may be time to relocate to an area in which that danger is absent.

If you are located in an area in which you won't be jailed or otherwise legally punished for your lack of belief—but fear more intimate and emotional reprisals—it may be a good idea to seek professional

* *Annual Report of the United States Commission on International Religious Freedom, May 2009.*

counseling in the form of therapy or psychological treatment. This can be very helpful for those individuals interested in coming out, as well as those who have already faced discrimination from loved ones and hope to talk to someone about the issues religion has caused in his or her life.

It is important, though, that the therapist you choose isn't going to reinforce the negative stigma of nontheism or otherwise try to reconvert you—there are many "doctors" who are affiliated with a particular religion and see their sole responsibility as reconversion, as opposed to helping the struggling individual with their problems. To help provide a network of secular therapists, Dr. Darrel W. Ray, author of *The God Virus* and founder of Recovering from Religion, created the Secular Therapy Project. Here's an excerpt from the group's website describing what that organization is all about:

> *There are many secular people in your community that have mental health needs. Unfortunately, many secularists report that they cannot find a secular counselor in their community. We know there are often many secular therapists, but they cannot openly advertise as secular for fear of losing clients or other negative social and professional consequences. By registering you increase the likelihood that secular clients will find you and they will be able to avoid therapists who allow their religious,*

spiritual or supernatural beliefs to inform their therapeutic approach.*

The Secular Therapy Project is a unique answer to a common problem, and there are other similar secular projects being formed every day. And with an increasing number of atheists coming out across the world, we should expect this trend to continue. After all, the only way that these new nonreligious services can arise is if an entrepreneur sees a sufficient need.

---

* Secular Therapy Project, http://www.seculartherapy.org.

13

RELIGION AND GRIEF

You want a physicist to speak at your funeral. You want the physicist to talk to your grieving family about the conservation of energy, so they will understand that your energy has not died . . . You can hope your family will examine the evidence and satisfy themselves that the science is sound and that they'll be comforted to know your energy's still around. According to the laws of the conservation of energy, not a bit of you is gone; you're just less orderly.*

—AARON FREEMAN, PHYSICIST, AUTHOR OF
EULOGY FROM A PHYSICIST

One of the therapeutic benefits of spirituality is the hope that the idea of an afterlife sometimes instills in

---

* This is an excerpt from a longer quote by Aaron Freeman, American journalist, stand-up comedian, author, cartoonist, and blogger.

those experiencing grief from a loss. If you lose a loved one, and you truly believe that you'll see that person again in heaven, the argument can be made that the religious person's mentality provides a sort of peace with the loss. However, this can also work in reverse.

Regardless of your religious beliefs, you should never tell a mourning mother that it was "God's plan." For some people, that can be worse than saying nothing at all. For a nonbeliever, the words that are meant to console a religious person can do quite the opposite. A mother who loses her son, for example, might not wish to hear that God took her child or that she might see him as an "angel" someday—she probably just wants her son back. At the very best, this type of language is irrelevant and not applicable to atheists or anybody who doesn't subscribe to that particular worldview.

Holly Samel was nineteen years old when she found out she was pregnant. She was excited about the pregnancy and was already a couple of months along. She and her husband went to the hospital for an ultrasound—it was a boy. But, she said, the ultrasound technologist was acting suspiciously.

"She kept measuring stuff over and over," Holly said. "I was in there for more than an hour, and she said he was moving around too much—I asked her what was wrong, but it wasn't her job to tell me."

Holly and her husband left the ultrasound without being told any specifics, but they were happy. She began to call everyone she knew to tell them that her unborn child was a boy. Just as she was hanging up the phone after giving her mother the good news, her excitement quickly turned to immeasurable sorrow. Holly got the call from her midwife.

"She told me he wasn't going to make it. I started crying instantly," Holly said. "I have never felt anything that fast or real before. Even in my most uncontrolled emotional moment, I did not lean on religion. I had been nonreligious my whole life. It never even crossed my mind that it could help me out."

Holly later found out that her son had a rare form of dwarfism that meant his bones were improperly developed, coupled with other genetic defects—he wouldn't survive. Holly was five months pregnant at the time.

"They offered me an abortion because there was absolutely no chance of him making it, but I chose to continue the pregnancy," Holly said. "My midwife allowed me to come in and listen to his heartbeat as often as I wanted. I wanted to keep what I had with him as long as I could. The stress put me into early labor anyway when I was almost six months along, and Ethan weighed 1.9 pounds. Looking back at how tiny and frail he was, plus the religious sympathies getting to me, I started to think about what they could possibly think heaven would be like for him. I kept wondering who would care for him, or if they feel he wouldn't need care in heaven. They all wanted to tell me how sure they were he was now in heaven having a good afterlife, but no one had the details about it that I craved."

Since that time, people told Holly many things about her experience—especially the typical "comforting" statements: "He's in a better place now," or "It was part of God's plan," or that God (for whatever reason) "needed Ethan."

Although she wasn't religious, she just ignored the statements at first. She knew they meant well. That stayed true until a few years later, when her own grandmother said something that Holly couldn't ignore.

"She found out I was an atheist and emailed me. She said she knew that I had to believe in heaven because I want to see my son again. She said my atheism was just a phase," Holly recalled. "She had the same thing happen to her first son. I couldn't help but think that it has been more than forty years since she lost her son and every day she's needed to believe she is going to see him in heaven. It has been only five years since I lost Ethan, and I never needed a similar comfort on my worst days. I feel like atheism or a nonreligious grieving process allows you to deal with the death more honestly."

Holly wanted to learn more about how and why this happened to her son.

"I asked the midwife to explain to me as best she can," Holly said. "I was confused, and I didn't believe that he really had no chance. They told me the science behind why he couldn't have lived and about how horrible his life would have been if he had."

If anything, the experience reinforced her atheism. She knew that no all-loving and all-powerful God would allow this type of injustice—not just for her but for the millions in similar situations around the world.

In the end, what really helped Holly were logical explanations of her son's genetic disabilities, and not the false hope that religion offers. Holly said, with the complexities of religious portrayals of afterlife, assuming a pre-birth child is in heaven, there's no telling whether or not that would even be a good thing. Would he be a fetus in heaven? Would he grow? Who would care for him? Would he go to hell? She said none of it made sense—and scientific explanations and reason helped her through the grief.

For those nonbelievers experiencing the death of a loved one, there is no more prominent support group than Grief Beyond Belief. Grief Beyond Belief is an online support network for people grieving the death of a child, parent, partner, or other loved one—without belief in a higher power or any form of afterlife. Atheists, agnostics, humanists, freethinkers, and anyone else living without religious beliefs are invited to participate. Grief Beyond Belief was launched by Rebecca Hensler after the death of her three-month-old son.*

---

* https://www.facebook.com/faithfreegriefsupport.

14

FREQUENTLY ASKED QUESTIONS

Who questions much, shall learn much, and
retain much.

—FRANCIS BACON,
PHILOSOPHER AND STATESMAN

In this chapter, I will lay out some of the questions I'm
asked most often as a secular advocate—along with a
brief response for each one. The answers are my own
and do not necessarily apply to every nonbeliever. But
they do give a look into my worldview, most specifically
that of an atheist and naturalist. As an atheist coming
out, you will no doubt encounter some of these same
questions. My hope is that my responses will help provide some insights into your own answers as well as
more clearly understand my motivations and intentions.

Q: I know you don't believe in the Christian God, but
do you believe in other gods or the devil?

A: I don't believe in any supernatural or paranormal beings, forces, or entities simply because there is no evidence for their existence. I also don't believe in magic, superstition, or astrology. I would, however, be open to changing my mind—for the right evidence.

Q: Do you know there is no God?

A: No, I don't claim absolute certainty on the nonexistence of gods . . . but uncertainty should never be enough to warrant belief. Nobody knows absolutely how we got here, but I'm more comfortable with following the scientific evidence on the subject than I am in proclaiming the existence of a deity or deities out of my own ignorance of the facts. Depending on how you define "god," the existence of one ranges from highly improbable and unnecessary to nearly impossible—but if you define God as the prayer-answering deity of the Abrahamic religions that interferes with earthly affairs, it is fairly easy to conclude that it likely does not exist. If there is a deity, it is completely detached. It has used methods of creation that are indistinguishable from nature, it has declined to make itself known for all of recorded history, it doesn't interfere with earthly matters, and has made itself impossible to observe. There is no evidence for such a being, and its existence is improbable and unnecessary at best, but even if you believe in that god . . . why would you think it would want to be worshipped?

Q: Why did you decide to become an atheist?

A: I never "decided" to become an atheist—and, in fact, I don't think belief or nonbelief is something you necessarily choose. In my case, I simply followed the evidence. The question presupposes that theism or religiosity is the natural state, which it is not. We are all born free from all religious affiliations and only come to believe in such things after being introduced to it—so, atheism is the default position. Although some children are not indoctrinated with a specific religion before the age of reason, there are many more who are—I was lucky in that my religious upbringing didn't stick. I never believed in gods or goddesses because I've never seen evidence to support such claims. For me, everything has always been explainable in natural terms, so assigning a deity or deities to anything seemed counter-productive, especially when the attributes of the deity aren't even agreed upon by its own followers—and believers use their god to justify what they think is right and to condemn what they think is wrong. Because the existence of deities is both highly improbable and unnecessary, taking the leap of faith to believe in one simply never occurred to me.

Q: There is a God-shaped void in your heart. Don't you feel that your life is missing something without God?

A: If such a God exists, there must be a glitch in its system . . . I'm very happy. I do what I love, I have an amazing family, I do good for others when I can, and I'm not hindered in the least bit by not believing in deities. There is no void. In fact, I'm quite happy that I don't fear death. An eternity of anything could eventually be torture, and I'm happy to live my life to its fullest without regard to the possibility of a second.

Q: What would it take to change your mind?

A: The only thing that would change my mind is concrete evidence. If there were substantial testable, peer-reviewed evidence that showed that the presence of a deity was highly probable or required for anything on earth, I'd certainly be subject to reevaluating my position. But that will never happen because of the very nature of all deities—and all things supernatural; at the end of the day, a believer has to rely on faith. If in some radical miracle, the Abrahamic God revealed his existence to the world, I'd accept the belief in the deity—but I still wouldn't worship it. The jealous and angry God that justified the killings of millions, sent plagues upon firstborns, and abhorred homosexuals would not be worthy of my worship.

Q: Why do you dislike believers and/or religion?

A: I don't dislike believers. The average believer, while arguably gullible, is guilty of nothing more than wishful thinking. I don't even dislike religions; they can be very interesting from a phenomenological and historical approach. But when religion justifies violence, impedes scientific progress, and gives motivation to strip people of human rights, I feel that criticism is warranted and necessary. But my critiques shouldn't be confused with disdain; pointing out the negative aspects of religion and inconsistencies within belief systems does not equate to hatred or persecution.

Q: Why don't you believe just in case we are right? What do you have to lose? ["If you gain, you gain all. If you lose, you lose nothing. Wager then, without hesitation, that He exists."—Pascal's wager]

A: I can't simply will myself to believe; belief doesn't work that way. I don't believe in gods not because I don't want to but because all the evidence points to the contrary—and I don't accept things on faith. Belief without evidence just doesn't compute for me. So, I suppose I could pretend to believe, but do you think that feigned belief resulting from a fear of hell would make one worthy of heaven to an all-knowing God? Salvation usually requires genuine acceptance of a deity, and that's something I cannot give for any radical claim without substantial supporting evidence. Even if I were to genuinely accept a deity, though, which religion is the "right" one? From Bahá'í to Buddhism to Wicca to Zoroastrianism, hundreds of religions with thousands of denominations exist globally today, and countless others have been cast aside over time, many of them claiming authority over the next. Accepting one god on faith would condemn me to all others—so, skepticism of all deities is the more prudent approach.

Q: You just don't understand religion because you have never felt God. Have you ever had a personal relationship with your Creator?

A: No, I've never been a believer. In fact, I've spent most of my life trying to figure out why people believe what they do. But I'm an exception to the much more common path to atheism; many nonbelievers (perhaps most in certain regions of the world) used to think they had a "personal relationship" with God . . . they "felt" God, and they were convinced of the power of prayer. Some were missionaries and clergymen because they wanted to do God's work, and some were simply indoctrinated with a religion while they were too young to think for themselves. Some people have switched religions—feeling the "power" of Allah and Jesus and other deities in one lifetime, but now they know that there is no personal relationship because there's nothing there. They concluded that prayer doesn't affect the external world, and they realized that any feelings created by the religion came from within and not from some external source.

Q: Can't God and religion coexist with science?

A: One would first have to define the "God" in question. There are millions of proposed deities that span across cultures and regions throughout human history. I wouldn't necessarily say that every god is fundamentally antiscience except in that they are all based on faith, which is by definition lacking the evidence that science could measure; belief in gods is directly opposed to scientific thought in that way. That being said, if you define God as the Abrahamic God with its affiliated holy texts—the prayer-answering Creator-God who is said to have spoken everything into existence and who supposedly interferes regularly with affairs on earth—then that God is certainly contrary to our progressing scientific understandings. A lot of the conflict between religion and science stems from the stagnancy of scripture; when the Bible is supposed to be the divinely inspired Word of God and then it makes ridiculous claims like that man was made from dirt and the earth was created in six days, you get generations of people who fight against our evolving understandings of our origins, often insisting creationism be taught in public schools. If you look at the organizations that have consistently impeded the progress of science, you'll see that they are most often religious in nature.

Q: You may not be religious, but don't you think our morals come from religion?

A: No, that's a common misconception. I feel sorry for anyone who thinks they need stone tablets to know not to murder, because it is simply not the case. What we now call *morality* has evolved—as nearly every physical and social human attribute has—to aid us in survival and, ultimately, reproduction. As a social species, ethical behavior within social interactions is necessary for our development. This morality requires that we be guided by a conscience (or "moral sense")—and not by a god or gods. Historically, founders of religions integrated moral prescriptions from their own time period and region into a religion's teachings as a way to emulate moral transcendence. The problem with this is not that the morals taught are inherently bad but that the holy books are stagnant in nature. Over time, our understanding of what is "moral" changes, but the words in the Bible, Qur'an, and so on do not to any great degree. Religions hinder our own moral evolution by teaching followers strict adherence to these archaic traditions. Using the Old Testament, it is easy to see how far we have come in that we no longer condone acts that were explicitly accepted (or commanded) during that period, such as the stoning of disobedient children and nonbelievers. Even in the New Testament, we have in large part outgrown the ideas of subservience of women and the discrimination of homosexuals as "sinners" who should burn in hell. It is important to understand that religions as moral guides can be quite dangerous once those morals are no longer relevant, especially when those "morals" teach discrimination against those who disagree. When all is said and done, the stagnant morals of any holy book will always work to inhibit our own moral evolution over time.

Q: What about the therapeutic benefits of religion?

A: I don't think religion is therapeutic at all, but it certainly doesn't accomplish anything that secular therapies cannot. The mentality that religion instills, while arguably comforting at times, does not help the believer solve his or her problems. Religion gives the illusion of therapy while actually shifting responsibilities for outcomes from the person to an unknowable deity—allowing any event to be chalked up to "God's plan." When a believer accomplishes something great and credits his or her accomplishments to a god, it takes away from the individual's hard work that is likely responsible and implies that person was somehow more important to God than anybody else who may have prayed equally and failed. And when a believer does something bad, religion grants salvation based solely on belief—allowing "divine" justification for any crime based solely on the unsubstantiated idea that faith forgives sins. "This life is only a test" is a counterproductive mindset; it encourages wishful thinking toward an elusive and likely nonexistent afterlife while often enabling the believer to squander this life as somehow less important.

Q: Isn't raising your children as atheists a form of religious indoctrination?

A: Since atheism is not a religion, the simple answer is *no*. But I wouldn't raise my children as atheists, although I expect that they would reach that conclusion on their own. I think it is important to give children a healthy dose of religious education early on, teaching them a broad range of comparative mythology and religion from a phenomenological approach. If you study comparative religion, it is harder to be religious because religions are all very similar at the fundamental level. Each organization has similar cult beginnings and prophets, they each began as local and cultural myths before being applied to a global context, and they are almost always spread through a combination of violence and proselytization. By learning about the origins of myths and the histories of various religious institutions, children can see all religions as part of the same phenomenon and not see one as inherently superior to all others.

Q: Aren't you just making science your God? Don't you have faith that science will always provide the right answers?

A: There is no room for faith in science. Literally defined as "belief without evidence," faith is the antithesis of the scientific method. In science, one is always looking for evidence, verifying data, and updating understandings. Therein lies the clash with most religions and science—the religious put their faith in a book or a teaching that claims transcendence, yet never lives up to it. Scientific findings are not always right, and that is thoroughly recognized. Actually, it is one of the best parts of how scientific understandings work because they are able to be changed and revised when a better idea comes along—scientists don't proclaim a hypothesis to be too sacred to be criticized and altered for better results. I don't have faith that science can provide all the answers because science already has the answers—the realities are there, we just have to discover them. We are far from done learning new things about the universe, but the moment you give up and have faith that some unknowable deity is responsible for everything is the moment that scientific curiosity and intellectual discovery are lost.

Q: If there is a heaven, would you want to go? Are you afraid that hell might be real?

A: Heaven and hell are logically flawed concepts. If you put an "eternity" into perspective, it is hard to imagine that where we supposedly go for an infinite period of time is based solely upon our actions (and beliefs) in a period of usually less than one hundred years on earth. Infinite torture in hell for any trespass on earth is unjustified. As a result of this logical conclusion and the fact that no evidence exists for any type of afterlife, I no more fear the Christian hell than a Christian fears the Muslim hell. However, if the Christian heaven and

hell are real and belief in Jesus is the only determin-
ing factor as to who is "saved," then heaven would be
a haven for repented rapists and murderers. Not only
would heaven be home to some of the worst criminals
in human history, but it would also be an eternity of deity worship apart from every person who held differing
religious beliefs, even if that person were someone you
loved deeply for your entire life. I don't want any part
of that paradise.

Q: If you aren't religious, why do you spend so much
time talking about and studying religion?

A: I've never been a religious person, but I've always
been interested in why people believe the things they
do. And I find religion—as a phenomenon—very interesting. I've always enjoyed learning about comparative
mythology, and modern mythologies are no different.
Through an education in religious studies, I learned
about the creation myths from various cultures and
those myths' earlier influences, about the similarities
and inconsistencies within each belief system, and how
each religion has grown—through a combination of
violence and proselytization—from a localized cult to
its modern global equivalent. The problems begin when
believers try to force their superstitions and beliefs on
others, either institutionally or through violence. While
extremists kill and die in the name of their religion,
so-called moderates fight for legislation to include

creationism in textbooks and, in America, work tirelessly to turn an explicitly secular nation into a Christian one. When believers use their religion as a tool to manipulate the education of children and destroy separation of church and state, it is absolutely imperative that secular advocates do their part.

Q: By talking about your atheism, aren't you pushing it on others? Why be vocal about it at all?

A: There is nothing wrong with talking about the fact that you're an atheist, and questions like this are oddly reminiscent of questions asked of homosexuals who are "too open" about who they are. Saying, "I'm an atheist," is no more confrontational than the religious identifiers used by believers. For example, in America, we have an abundance of all things Christian, from door-to-door missionaries, megachurches, and WWJD bumper stickers to Ichthys (Jesus Fish) and crucifixes on the necks of men, women, and children—people proclaim, "I'm a Christian!" in more ways than I can count. Unfortunately for me and many atheists, theism and religiosity are the assumed points of view in many cultures, and vocal disagreement with the status quo often results in discrimination. Atheists aren't the ones knocking on doors selling their particular brand of "truth." Atheists don't have massive tax-exempt organizations with influential political action committees dedicated to atheism. And, most importantly, atheists don't insist that everyone who disagrees with them will burn in hell for eternity.

Q: God is like the wind—you can't see it, but you know it exists. Why do you believe in wind and not God?

A: I don't believe in gods not because they're invisible but because there's absolutely no evidence of any earthly object or force that points directly to any Supreme Being—or for anything supernatural, for that matter. God is not like the wind—we can clearly and accurately measure the routes of wind patterns and, when winds become potentially dangerous by forming severe weather systems, we can see the wind's movements and understand the forces that generate them. We can feel its forces and scientifically understand why they are there. If I notice a tree is blown over into the road after a storm, I may conclude that the wind is to blame—but there is no action that can be attributed to a "God." There exists chance and good outcomes and bad outcomes, but no outcomes that need be attributed to acts of God. God's force is nothing like wind because there is no force to describe.

Q: Why do you do what you do? What is the point of advocating for secularism?

A: I think that we can make a legitimate difference by showing closet nonbelievers that they're not alone and by educating the religious about the flaws and negative impacts of the belief systems that they've (often un-wittingly) dedicated their lives to. Some people spend their entire lives devoted to a religion that claims to be the "right" religion. They often deny scientific evidence that contradicts their archaic holy books, they some-times oppress those who disagree with them, and they always do what they do in the name of an unknowable deity . . . but sometimes, they wake up. Occasionally, they realize that all religions are man-made and that none of them are "right." And when they do, they can live happy and fulfilling lives without dogma and with-out anticipating or fearing an afterlife. If I can play any small role in the process of helping people to live an honester life, then I've done my job.

Q: If you don't believe in God, what's the meaning of life?

A: In my opinion, the only constant in life—including nonhuman life—the only objective "meaning" is the innate urge to protect and preserve one's own blood-line. That being said, as an atheist, I don't claim to know an overarching meaning of life. I think that life is only what you make of it. I operate under the understanding that this life shouldn't be lived under the pretense that it is simply a test propagated by an invisible, intangible Creator-God. And it should not be spent identifying with religious traditions and or-ganized groups that, historically, have been at the root of a tremendous amount of oppression and violence. It is my sincere opinion that our precious time on earth should not be spent attempting to justify unbelievable acts of cruelty, death, and disease as a part of "God's plan" or the greater good—and clinging to ancient texts that preach ill-concealed bigotry and sexism. Instead, we should find ways to make this life happy and satisfying, without regard to the unknowable nature of an afterlife.

Q: Are you scared to read the Bible because you know that, if you did, you'd believe like I do?

A: Personally, I'm not scared to read the Bible at all. In fact, I have a degree in religious studies with an emphasis on Christianity and Mediterranean traditions, and I've read the Bible from front to back more times than I can count. But it doesn't make the case for a deity, as you seem to believe. What we know as the Bible is actually dozens of books by mostly anonymous authors that have been compiled together over several generations and by a variety of complex political mechanisms and secret councils. As a result, it is riddled with contradictions and inaccuracies, especially between books. This has actually made the Bible one of the biggest recruiters of new atheists, who in many cases read the Bible looking for answers or for inspiration, and instead come away losing their faith, often a key piece of one's identity. Anecdotally, I saw this with fellow religious studies majors in college. And scientifically, studies have shown that atheists and nonbelievers are more informed about religion than most religious denominations.

That being said, although it helps, one doesn't have to read the Bible to be an atheist any more than one would have to read the Qur'an or the Bhagavad Gita to be a Christian. All one needs to be an atheist is a basic knowledge of how the world works and an understanding that "God did it" isn't an acceptable answer to how it got that way.

Q: I happen to know that all religions are equally true. Have you considered that the different traditions are all different paths to the same God figure?

A: I have definitely considered that notion, and I applaud the attempt to be inclusive and to promote a sense of equality and unity among world faiths. Unfortunately, the position can be debunked rather easily when you consider the contradictory wishes and impulses of every deity to ever be conceived. For example, Islam generally teaches that Christians will go to hell, while Christianity says the same thing about Muslims. Both gods can't be real because they'd have competing realities. Now consider the fact that those are actually the same Abrahamic deity. "Allah" is just another word for "God," and both figures share the same origin in the Jewish scriptures. So, if two interpretations of one single god can't coexist, then what does that say about the thousands of deities who are currently worshipped? Or of all the gods who have ever been worshipped? It's not possible.

Q: Do you really believe the universe just came from nothing? That's impossible.

A: Atheists don't necessarily believe the universe "came from nothing," but there are some well-known scientists who have theories on just that. Although it's a bit complexer than this, it can be boiled down to gravity and the laws of physics. In other words, according to some celebrated thinkers, the universe's creation was essentially an inevitability. So, scientific theories do posit a creator-less universe, but can the same be said for a Creator? Not even close. There are zero scientific theories for how an all-knowing, all-loving, and all-powerful deity—a concept infinitely complexer than an otherwise empty universe—could have arisen from nothing at all, or from gravity. If we assume either the universe or God had to come from nothing, it makes more sense to conclude that it was the universe.

Q: What do you think will happen to you when you die?

A: The evidence points to one answer: nothing. It hurts to hear, because we are humans who have an uncomfortable awareness of the fact that we will die, and an afterlife would be nice. But wanting something to be true doesn't make it so. To be more objective about this question, I like to encourage people to think about what happens to fish or fungus when they die. These, like humans, are living beings, yet humans typically have no problem imagining that these creatures simply cease to exist after they die. We are just animals; there's no reason to believe anything special happens to us after death, and any other position is contrary to all evidence. What we know for sure with all animals is that our brains stop functioning and our hearts stop pumping, and then our bodies decompose. We do, however, live on in the memories we leave with loved ones and in our achievements here on earth.

Q: I don't want you to go to hell. Can I pray for you to find God?

A: Of course you can! You can pray all you want—I can't and wouldn't want to stop you—but it stands to reason that other Christians would have done the same, meaning that your attempts would be duplicative and therefore unnecessary because other believers have tried it without any success. In fact, I find it pretty hard to believe a real god would need prayers to inform it of anything. So, while I won't try to stop you from praying for me, I would humbly request a good deed instead. After all, if for every well-intended prayer uttered in hopes of making the world a better place, there was instead a good deed accomplished, the world might look as though those prayers had been answered.

Q: I'm fine with you not believing in a religion, but do you have to shove your atheism down our throats?

A: You don't want atheism shoved down your throat? OK. We will stop knocking on doors spreading our "truth" and having tax-exempt organizations dedicated to atheism that have influential political action committees. We will also stop printing *IN ATHEISM WE TRUST* on all US currency and saying, "One nation, under atheism," in the Pledge of Allegiance. We will also stop insisting that everyone who disagrees with us will be sentenced to eternal damnation . . . Wait, that's not how this works at all. Because atheists are a tiny minority, there is no amount of openness about it that causes a problem for society. Christianity will always be pushed in your face more than atheism ever could, at least in the United States, so atheists should be allowed to be open about their ideas like everyone else.

Q: Don't you think it's a little narcissistic to believe that there is no God up there watching over us?

A: No. In fact, I think it's slightly more self-centered to be so absolutely sure that you are built in the image of an all-powerful Creator-God, and that same God answers your prayers, knows your name, and has a personal relationship with you. Nonbelief actually represents a less human-centric view of the world.

That's not to say, however, that believers are necessarily narcissistic; belief has nothing to do with that. All this says is that human beings in general tend to seek out higher powers and that we tend to model unknown figures after what we do know. This is why most descriptions of aliens are humanoid in nature, standing on two legs with eyes that face forward.

Q: I'm a Christian, and I believe God is very real, so humor me for a moment. If you die and you are standing before Him, what would you say?

A: I'd say, "Why did you feel the need to commit mass genocides, condone slavery, and promote the subjugation of women? And why does your inspired book indicate that the world is less than ten thousand years old and that man was created from dirt and women of his rib when common sense and scientific facts tell us otherwise? Why do you have to rely on faith to believe in you—and why is that the same for every religion? Why did you used to perform grandiose miracles but, since the inception of modern recording devices, absolutely stop? Why is there no evidence of any supernatural entity, let alone a prayer-answering God? Why has prayer—in every scientific study—been shown to do absolutely nothing? Why would you cause more than two-thirds of your creations—your 'children'—to burn for eternity simply for being unconvinced of your existence or being born into a culture that worships a 'false God'? Why would you have one 'chosen' people over every other group and culture across all of human history? Why would you create evil in the first place? Why didn't you need a creator?"

Q: Why do atheists seem so angry at God and Christians and Jesus?

A: You should be careful of stereotyping, as I'm an atheist and don't express anger or disdain for Christians or Christianity, let alone at God or Jesus. In fact, I think that logical discourse and reasonable discussion work much better than ridicule and aggression. After all, most believers aren't dumb—they are likelier simply indoctrinated with irrational beliefs through no fault of their own. This is not to mention that there are Christians who seem to be equally angry, if not angrier. See Westboro Baptist Church for a prime example of this type of Christian hatred, although there are many others. This is why it's important not to judge a group based on the actions of a few.

Atheists are certainly not angry with God or Jesus, as these are fictional characters to a nonbeliever. It would be like asking why Christians are so angry with Thor, Zeus, and Muhammad. It just doesn't make sense. An atheist can, however, be angry with the injustices of religion or with the infiltration of one religion or another into legislation. In America, for example, Christianity is the predominant religion. As a result, "Christian" ideals permeate through our laws resulting in various infringements upon our secular nation's supposed separation of church and state. This can come in something as harmless as *IN GOD WE TRUST* being printed on all American legal tender or as harsh as denying homosexuals civil rights based on that religion's principles. Christianity has resulted in creationism and false sciences being taught in our public schools and has been the main impediment of potentially lifesaving stem cell research. All in all, I can see why some nonbelievers would be angry over such injustices in a government that is supposed to be free from the influences of religion.

Q: Why do so many atheists want others to reject the existence of God?

A: Personally, I don't care if others "reject the existence of God." I do, however, want people to ask questions about ideas with which they may have been indoctrinated as children. Even if those questions only reaffirm an individual's faith, I think the act of questioning is a virtue in itself. I also want them to be able to think about and discuss topics that are generally considered taboo, because that's how we learn and grow as a society. There should be nothing so sacred that it can't be questioned or even talked about. Further, I feel that religions in many instances get a free pass in society, so I think it's important to shine a light on them. So, there are a number of reasons why I write about these contro-versial issues, including faith. And I'm sure many other atheists feel similarly.

Q: If Christianity isn't the truth, how did it spread all around the world while other religions haven't?

A: Christianity owes a lot of its success to colonization and forced conversions centuries ago, but that's not even the primary reason it has been so successful in spread-ing. Think about it for a second. If you want your reli-gion to be widely accepted, what would you do? You'd make it so that the worst sin is refusal to propagate it. Not rape. Not murder. But the mere act of being un-convinced. That's exactly what Christianity does, and it's a tool that allows it to go further.

So is the entire concept of hell and "eternal salva-tion." Again, if you want your religion to spread, what do you do? You make people think they'll go to hell if they don't spread it and be rewarded with bliss if they do. Further than that, you tell them that their children and grandchildren will suffer eternally if they aren't indoctrinated with this same belief! It works like a charm.

This might seem like bad news, but think about that last part. If none of that is real, your children and grand-children *aren't* at risk of being punished forever based not on their actions but on their beliefs. They won't be arbitrarily struck down by a being that, by definition, designed the system in the first place, including hell and Satan. To me, that seems pretty nice.

Q: You may not believe the Bible is holy or inspired by God, but do you believe it's true? Many scholars seem to recognize the Bible as nonfiction.

A: Christian scholars might consider the Bible "non-fiction," but, like all so-called holy books, it contains a mixture of historical anecdotes and unconfirmed (and unfalsifiable) magical tales. The books of the Bible were written by a number of different people, over many years, and therefore their content varies. In general, we have been able to verify the existence of certain characters and minor events, but they are almost always exaggerated or altered based on the perception of the writer—primarily due to the lack of primary sources. On the other hand, some biblical claims (such as many of those made in Exodus) have been extensively debunked and are entirely fictional. As I've said in the past, holy books often have a kernel of truth mixed in with the "divine" stories, which is really the only way the religions would be accepted on a large scale. I hope that helps clear things up!

15

CONCLUSION

A conclusion is the place where you got tired
of thinking.

—Martin H. Fischer, doctor and writer

Being openly nonreligious is unreasonably tough in
many societies. It seems that, in some areas, faith is
thought to trump reason—an idea that, while under-
standably present in most sacred scriptures that seek to
glorify belief and worship, doesn't make sense if you actually think about it. And the fact that we prefer critical
thought over blind faith doesn't make nonbelievers bad
people. It doesn't make us any likelier to lie, cheat, steal,
or murder, according to every study.

So, when a person takes offense to someone else's
conclusion that gods likely don't exist, it tells us more
about the believer than the atheist. And whether that
response is a result of their own insecurities of faith
or preconceived notions about atheists, it's possible to

improve the situation. If discriminatory believers see in practice that atheism does not affect one's ability to act ethically and maintain a happy and full life, perhaps some of the prejudices will fall away over time.

I hope that the narratives and advice given in this guide to speaking to others about atheism are helpful for those who may be suffering from persecution as a result of their nonbelief, but also those who simply want to learn about the process of leaving faith behind or even to find and connect with like-minded thinkers. Helping to dispel the myths of nonbelief among many religious communities is an important task, and with more people deciding to take the crucial step of declaring their disbelief than ever, believers are likely to see that *atheist* is not synonymous with *Satanist,* and that nonbelievers are not "god-hating sinners." People will start to see that their neighbors or children or dentists don't see evidence for belief in archaic superstitions, and they are still good people, so maybe it is not that bad after all.

While this book may not be all one needs to successfully come out as an atheist, I hope that it helps guide nonbelievers young and old throughout that ongoing process. For me, what helped most to deal with any instance of religious discrimination was to understand religious mindset and the specific intricacies of religious belief. If you understand the historical and cultural aspects of religion, it can help you to comprehend not just what people believe but why they believe it and how they come to be so firmly held in that particular mindset. This understanding, perhaps above all else, can help one to navigate the negative interactions that are all too often part of being openly atheistic.

The fact will always remain that people—more often than not—inherit their religious beliefs from parents or childhood mentors. The familial indoctrination that achieves the startling success rate of religious transmission begins with childhood baptisms, forced participation in religious rituals from a young age, and teaching children who are too young to understand that their religion is the only correct one, and that all others will burn in hell. Once the child is old enough to think logically about the possible veracity of various religions, it is often too late—the religious instruction has been so successful that the child no longer accepts the possibility that they could be wrong.

There is admittedly a trend in religious practice toward the more liberal versions of the traditions. As discussed previously, in the United States, I've noticed a move toward cultural Christianity. While these people may consider themselves "Christians," it is sometimes in name only. They often know extraordinarily little about the tradition or its origins and instead identify with it out of cultural familiarity and fear of the unknown. But there is also a separate group of religious people in the world today—they are often pushing back against the liberalization of their religion and the growing secularization of first-world nations. These hyper-religious zealots are the Islamic terrorists proclaiming jihad against the Westerners and the fundamentalist Christians bombing abortion clinics. They are advocates for Young Earth creationism being taught in public schools, and they preach scripture before science and faith before reason. It is with these individuals that the tide of abuse and discrimination against nonbelievers is most prominent.

The narratives and stories shared in this work are personal and true testimonies that are intended to aid other individuals who may be facing similar situations. I'd like to sincerely thank our contributors; without them, this work could not provide the wide range of viewpoints on the topic of de-conversion. Whether you've recently de-converted or you've been an atheist for years and never experienced a problem, I hope this guide provided some insight into the views of those nonbelievers who are oppressed, as well as some resources to build a community with individuals who, like you, have decided that the best religion is no religion.

RESOURCES AND SUPPORT

What spectacle can be more edifying or
more seasonable, than that of Liberty and
Learning, each leaning on the other for their
mutual and surest support?

—JAMES MADISON (MARCH 16, 1751–JUNE
28, 1836)

For members of the LGBTQ community, coming out is
an established practice. In fact, there is a lot that atheists can learn from that community regarding when,
where, and how to come out. For those who identify
as LGBTQ, for example, there are a host of websites,
books, documentaries, social networks, counseling
programs, and more to aid in the most difficult aspects
of coming out to less-than-understanding family and
friends. Some programs include the Human Rights
Campaign's Resource Guide and AVERT HIV & AIDS

charity. For nonbelievers, there are also a variety of support programs, although perhaps not nearly enough. Here I will compile a list of various resources for the nonreligious—including blogs, social networks, and advocacy programs, as well as a directory of helpful secular organizations—from throughout North America. These resources should be helpful to any nonbeliever— and not necessarily just those who come from unsupportive or fundamentalist families.

Secular Advocacy Groups and Organizations

AMERICAN ATHEISTS: Founded in 1963, American Atheists is an organization laboring for the civil liberties of atheists and the absolute separation of government and religion. Created by Madalyn Murray O'Hair, the noted atheist activist, American Atheists is dedicated to working for the civil rights of atheists, promoting separation of state and church, and providing information about atheism.

Website: www.atheists.org
Email: info@atheists.org
Physical Headquarters: 225 Cristiani Street, Cranford, NJ 07016
Phone Number: (908) 276-7300

AMERICAN HUMANIST ASSOCIATION: The mission of the American Humanist Association is to be a clear, democratic voice for humanism in the United States, to increase public awareness and acceptance of humanism, to establish, protect, and promote the position of humanists in our society, and to develop and advance humanist thought and action.

Website: www.americanhumanist.org
Email: aha@americanhumanist.org
Physical Headquarters: 1821 Jefferson Place, NW, Washington, D.C. 20036
Phone Number: (202) 238-9088

AMERICANS UNITED FOR SEPARATION OF CHURCH AND STATE: Americans United (AU) represents members and supporters in all fifty states and is dedicated to preserving the constitutional principle of church-state separation as the only way to ensure religious freedom for all. AU is a 501(c)(3) non-profit educational organization based in Washington, D.C. Founded in 1947, Americans United works in the courts, in Congress and state legislatures, at the White House, and in the arena of public opinion.

Website: www.au.org
Email: americansunited@au.org
Physical Headquarters: 1310 L Street NW, Suite 200, Washington, D.C. 20005
Phone Number: (202) 466-3234

ATHEIST ALLIANCE INTERNATIONAL: The mission of Atheist Alliance International (AAI) is to challenge and confront religious organizations and faith, and strengthen global atheism by promoting the growth and interaction of atheist and free thought organizations in countries and regions around the world, and by undertaking international educational and advocacy projects.

Website: www.atheistalliance.org
Email: info@atheistalliance.org
Physical Headquarters: 216 Mt. Herman Road,
Suite #178, Scotts Valley, CA 95066

ATHEISTS OF FLORIDA: Atheists of Florida, Inc. is a registered 501(c)(3) organization that's affiliated with American Atheists. The group, which is primarily concerned with fighting for the separation of church and state, was founded in 1992.

Website: www.atheistsofflorida.org
Email: admin@Atheistsofflorida.org
Physical Headquarters: PO Box 130753,
Tampa, FL 33681 USA

BLACK NONBELIEVERS: Black Nonbelievers, Inc. is a 501(c)(3) nonprofit organization dedicated to connecting with Blacks and allies who are free of faith but who "might otherwise be shunned by family and friends."

Website: https://blacknonbelievers.com
Email: mandisa@blacknonbelievers.org
Physical Headquarters: PO Box 133351,
Atlanta, GA 30333

RESOURCES AND SUPPORT

CENTER FOR INQUIRY: New York–based Center for Inquiry (CFI) is a nonprofit educational organization. The mission of the Center for Inquiry is to foster a secular society based on science, reason, freedom of inquiry, and humanist values. Established in 1991 by philosopher and author Paul Kurtz, CFI has more than eighteen branches in the United States and thirty-nine worldwide.

> Website: www.centerforinquiry.net
> Email: info@centerforinquiry.net
> Physical Headquarters: 3965 Rensch Road, Amherst, NY 14228
> Phone Number: (716) 636-4869

CLERGY PROJECT: A private, online community for active and former clergy who no longer hold supernatural beliefs to support one another.

> Website: https://clergyproject.org
> Email: clergy@clergyproject.org
> Physical Headquarters: 8800 49th St. N. Ste. 311, Pinellas Park, FL 33782
> Phone Number: (607) 742-1214

COALITION OF REASON: The United Coalition of Reason is a nonprofit national organization that helps local nontheistic groups work together to achieve higher visibility, gain more members, and have a greater impact in their local areas.

> Website: www.unitedcor.org
> Email: Info@UnitedCoR.org

Physical Headquarters: 1012 14th Street NW, Suite 205, Washington, D.C. 20005

Phone Number: (202) 299-1091, ext. 202

EX-MORMON FOUNDATION OF NORTH AMERICA: A diverse community led by former or questioning Mormons dedicated to supporting those who are creating a life after Mormonism.

Website: http://exmormonfoundation.org

Email: Exmf-Board-Owner@yahoogroups.com

EX-MUSLIMS OF NORTH AMERICA: A 501(c)(3) nonprofit that was founded in 2013 to stand for the rights of those who leave Islam. EXMNA promotes acceptance of religious dissent and secular values, and its leaders seek to reduce discrimination against former Muslims.

Website: https://exmuslims.org

Email: info@exmuslims.org

FOUNDATION BEYOND BELIEF: Texas-based Foundation Beyond Belief is a 501(c)(3) charitable foundation created to focus, encourage, and demonstrate humanist generosity and compassion. They select and feature five charitable organizations per quarter, one in each of the following cause areas: Education, Poverty and Health, Human Rights, the Natural World, and Challenge the Gap (charities based on other worldviews).

Website: www.foundationbeyondbelief.org

Contact: www.foundationbeyondbelief.org/contact-us/

Physical Headquarters: 1940 Fountain View Drive #1126, Houston, TX 77057

FREEDOM FROM RELIGION FOUNDATION: The Freedom from Religion Foundation (FFRF) promotes the constitutional principle of separation of state and church and educates the public on matters relating to nontheism. Incorporated in 1978 in Wisconsin, the foundation is a national membership association of more than seventeen thousand freethinkers: atheists, agnostics, and skeptics of any pedigree. The foundation is a nonprofit, tax-exempt, educational organization under Internal Revenue Code 501(c)(3). FFRF and its staff attorneys act on numerous violations of separation of state and church on behalf of members and the public, including prayers in public schools, payment of funds for religious purposes, government funding of pervasively sectarian institutions, and the ongoing campaign against civil rights for women, gays, and lesbians led by churches. FFRF is led by copresidents Dan Barker and Annie Laurie Gaylor. Barker is a former minister, evangelist, and secular author. Gaylor is an author and executive editor of *Freethought Today*.

Website: www.ffrf.org
Contact: https://secure.ffrf.org/np/clients/ffrf/survey.jsp?surveyId=6
Physical Headquarters: PO Box 750, Madison, WI 53701
Phone Number: (608) 256-8900

GRIEF BEYOND BELIEF: Grief Beyond Belief is dedicated to providing peer-to-peer grief support for nonbelievers by providing evangelism-free environments for sharing among those grieving.

Website: http://griefbeyondbelief.org
Contact: http://griefbeyondbelief.org.contact-us/

HUMANIST HUB: The Humanist Hub, founded as the first-ever "humanist chaplaincy" at Harvard, works with atheists, agnostics, and allies to "create an inclusive new model for how humanists celebrate life" and make the world a better place.

Website: https://www.humanisthub.org
Email: info@harvardhumanist.org
Physical Headquarters: 1953 Massachusetts Avenue, Unit 400405, Cambridge, MA 02140

HUMANISTS INTERNATIONAL: Humanists International is the global representative body of the humanist movement, working to bring a variety of nonreligious organizations and individuals together under the humanist umbrella.

Website: https://humanists.international
Contact: https://humanists.international/about/contact-us
Physical Headquarters: United States: 1821 Jefferson Place NW, Washington, D.C. 20036

IDEAS BEYOND BORDERS: Ideas Beyond Borders is dedicated to sharing, translating, and promoting ideas that "foster critical thinking, civil rights, science, pluralism," and more. The group hopes to "bring to life a modern, pluralistic Middle East, led by the people of the region."

Website: https://www.ideasbeyondborders.org
Email: info@ideasbeyondborders.org
Physical Headquarters: 244 Fifth Avenue, Suite 2594, New York, NY 10001
Phone Number: (646) 844-4076

INTERFAITH YOUTH CORE: A national nonprofit aimed at helping American youth of different faiths bridge their differences and find common values while working together.

Website: http://www.ifyc.org
Email: info@ifyc.org
Physical Headquarters: 141 W Jackson Blvd., Suite 3200, Chicago, IL 60604
Phone Number: (312) 573-8825

INTERNATIONAL ASSOCIATION OF ATHEISTS INC.: The International Association of Atheists, a registered 501(c)(3) organization founded in 2020, describes itself on its website as a "coalition of atheist and atheist-friendly organizations working together to make secular humanist initiatives happen." Cofounded by three women, IAA sent forty-one orphans to school in the Congo and raised thousands of dollars for legal defense teams in the first four months after it was launched.

Website: https://www.internationalatheists.org
Email: info@internationalatheists.org

Physical Headquarters: PO Box 114, Summerland, BC, Canada V0H1Z0

JAMES RANDI EDUCATIONAL FOUNDATION: The James Randi Educational Foundation (JREF) was founded in 1996 to help people defend themselves from paranormal and pseudoscientific claims. The JREF offers a still-unclaimed million-dollar reward for anyone who can produce evidence of paranormal abilities under controlled conditions. Through scholarships, workshops, and innovative resources for educators, the JREF works to inspire this investigative spirit in a new generation of critical thinkers.

Website: www.randi.org

JW SUPPORT: JW Support is a support program dedicated to helping youths who are being raised as Jehovah's Witnesses but who have come to realize it is not the truth. The system helps children cope with their situation until they are able to leave the home.

Website: https://jw.support
Contact: https://jw.support/emotional-assistance

LGBTQ HUMANIST ALLIANCE: The LGBTQ Humanist Alliance works at the national level to build a network of LGBTQ humanists who are "devoted to compassionate activism." The group, which can trace its roots back to the formation of the LGBT Humanist Council in 2009, hopes to achieve full equality and social liberation of all LGBTQ people.

Website: https://www.lgbtqhumanists.org
Email: lgbtqhumanists@americanhumanist.org
Physical Headquarters: 1821 Jefferson Place NW, Washington, D.C. 20036
Phone Number: (202) 238-9088

MILITARY ASSOCIATION OF ATHEISTS AND FREETHINKERS: The Military Association of Atheists and Freethinkers (MAAF) is a community support network that connects military members from around the world with each other and with local organizations. In addition to community services, they take action to educate and train both the military and civilian communities about atheists in the military and the issues that they face. Where necessary, MAAF identifies, examines, and responds to insensitive practices that illegally promote religion over non-religion within the military or unethically discriminate against minority religions or differing beliefs. MAAF supports Constitutional State-Church Separation and First Amendment rights for all service members.

Website: www.militaryatheists.org
Email: community@militaryatheists.org
Physical Headquarters: 1821 Jefferson Place NW, Washington, D.C. 20036
Phone Number: (202) 656-MAAF (6223)

MILITARY RELIGIOUS FREEDOM FOUNDATION: The Military Religious Freedom Foundation is a nonprofit civil rights organization dedicated to making sure all members of the United States Armed Forces "fully receive the Constitutional guarantee of both freedom of religion and freedom from religion, to which they and all Americans are entitled."

Website: https://www.militaryreligiousfreedom.org
Email: info@militaryreligiousfreedom.org
Physical Headquarters: 13170-B Central Avenue SE, Suite 255, Albuquerque, NM 87123
Phone Number: (800) 736-5109

RECOVERING FROM RELIGION: Recovering from Religion is a nonprofit organization dedicated to providing multi-dimensional support and encouragement to individuals leaving their religious affiliations through the establishment, development, training, and educational support of local groups nationwide.

Website: www.recoveringfromreligion.org
Contact: recoveringfromreligion.org/contact
Physical Headquarters: 10940 Parallel Pkwy Suite K-145, Kansas City, KS 66109

SATANIC TEMPLE: The Satanic Temple is a nontheistic religious group that is recognized as a church but stands against the erosion of the wall of separation between church and state in the United States. Contrary to what you may assume based on the group's name, its members don't worship or believe in the literal character of Satan, and instead use the established character as a metaphor.

Website: https://thesatanictemple.com
Contact: https://thesatanictemple.com/pages/contact

SECULAR COALITION FOR AMERICA: The Secular Coalition for America is a 501(c)(4) advocacy organization whose purpose is to amplify the diverse and growing voice of the nontheistic community in the United States. The coalition is located in Washington, D.C.

Website: www.secular.org
Contact: www.secular.org/contact
Physical Headquarters: 1012 14th Street NW #205, Washington, D.C. 20005
Phone Number: (202) 299-1091

SECULAR LATINO ALLIANCE: The Secular Latino Alliance is a support group and one of the few safe spaces for Latino individuals who are secular. The alliance has affiliated meetups around the world.

Website: http://secularlatinos.weebly.com
Email: Secularlatino@gmail.com
Phone Number: (913) 283-4816

SECULAR STUDENT ALLIANCE: The mission of the Secular Student Alliance is to organize, unite, educate, and serve students and student communities that promote the ideals of scientific and critical inquiry, democracy, secularism, and human-based ethics. The Secular Student Alliance is a 501(c)(3) educational nonprofit. The advocacy group works to organize and empower nonreligious students around the country.

Website: www.secularstudents.org
Email: ssa@secularstudents.org
Physical Headquarters: PO Box 411477, Los Angeles, CA 90041
Phone Number: (614) 441-9588

SKEPTICS SOCIETY: The Skeptics Society is a nonprofit 501(c)(3) organization dedicated to scientific communication. It seeks out experts who investigate extraordinary claims, including paranormal beliefs and pseudoscience in general. The society also publishes *Skeptic* magazine.

Website: https://www.skeptic.com
Email: skepticssociety@skeptic.com
Physical Headquarters: PO Box 338, Altadena, CA 91001
Phone Number: (626) 794-3119

Shops and Services

ARROGANT ATHEIST: The Arrogant Atheist is a destination for atheist shirts and accessories. The shop also features an established atheist-themed blog and discussion forum. www.thearrogantatheist.com

ATHEIST SHOES: Atheist Shoes saw its start in 2012 via Kickstarter. Its founders wanted godless individuals to be more open about their nonbelief, so they carved the words "ICH BIN ATHEIST" onto the sole of a shoe. The response online was tremendous, and it led to a full-on homemade shoe company doing business all over the world. Feel free to place your order here: https://atheist.shoes

ATHEIST REPUBLIC STORE: Atheist Republic is a growing community of godless heathens who share their views and discuss news, books, and ideas to help make life better. The advocacy group has dozens of items in its store: https://www.atheistrepublic.com/store

BLACKCRAFT CULT: Anaheim-based BlackCraft Cult was founded in an attic in the summer of 2012 by two individuals, Jim Somers and Bobby Schubenski, who believe you don't need God or organized religion to be a good person and do positive things for others. https://www.blackcraftcult.com

EVOLVEFISH: A Colorado-based enterprise that is dedicated to countering the destructive aspects of religious zealotry. They create and gather enlightened symbols and materials and advertise these products online, focusing on areas where zealots are trying to usurp the freedoms of the targets of their bigotry. www.evolvefish.com

GODLESS MOM: Godless Mom, founded by Courtney Heard of the International Association of Atheists, provides trendy designed clothes promoting secular values. www.godlessmom.com

HUMANIST SOCIETY: The Humanist Society lists celebrants who conduct secular wedding, naming, and death ceremonies at thehumanistsociety.org.

LOGIKAL THREADS: A small group of friends and family founded Logikal Threads to help nonbelievers express themselves and encourage others to question their religious beliefs. As a brand dedicated to free thought, free speech, and humanism, they also promote other important causes, such as vaccine awareness. www.logikalthreads.com

SECULAR THERAPY PROJECT: Part of Recovering from Religion, the Secular Therapy Project serves as a network through which secular individuals can find therapists who use nonreligious methods. www.seculartherapy.org

Blogs and Magazines

American Atheist magazine: A publication by American Atheists, *AA* magazine provides quarterly updates on what's going on in the atheist community. The organization was founded by Madalyn Murray O'Hair.

Atheist Revolution: A blog for people who are tired of irrational belief and religious extremism. It covers a variety of relevant topics. www.atheistrev.com

Debunking Christianity: A counter-apologetics blog by former Christian John W. Loftus, an atheist author who has earned three master's degrees from Lincoln Christian Seminary and Trinity Evangelical Divinity School. www.debunking -christianity.com

Faithless Feminist: Faithless Feminist features multiple writers who focus on the lives of women who leave be-

hind their patriarchal, faith-based institutions. www
.faithlessfeminist.com

Friendly Atheist: *Friendly Atheist* is a blog by Hemant Mehta,
speaker, math teacher, and author of *I Sold My Soul on eBay*.
https://friendlyatheist.patheos.com

Godless Mom blog: *Godless Mom* is a blog on Patheos and is
one of the most popular secular parenting blogs anywhere
online. Led by Courtney Heard, the blog features information and advice on current events and parenting generally.
www.patheos.com/blogs/godlessmom

Laughing in Disbelief: Andrew Hall hosts satirical secular news
blog *Laughing in Disbelief*, which he compares to *The On-
ion* on bath salts. www.patheos.com/blogs/laughingindis
belief

No Longer Quivering: A blog from the perspective of women
who left the Quiverfull movement, a conservative Christian
paradigm that encourages families to have as many children
as possible. www.patheos.com/blogs/nolongerquivering

No Sacred Cows: This is my own blog where I share secular
articles, essays, and ideas. https://www.patheos.com/blogs
/nosacredcows

Reddit-Atheism: The atheism subreddit is one of the most
popular places for nonbelievers to share news and studies
about religion and atheism. www.reddit.com/r/atheism

Skeptic magazine: A magazine dedicated to examining extraordinary claims and promoting science and reason. www .skeptic.com

Skeptical Inquirer: Skeptical Inquirer, a magazine for the Committee of Skeptical Inquiry. www.csicop.org/publications

Podcasts and Shows

Atheist Experience: The Atheist Experience is a weekly cable access and online TV show from Austin, Texas geared toward a nontheist audience. www.atheist-experience.com

The Bible Says What!?: *The Bible Says What!?* is an atheist versus Christian–style show including one-on-one conversations between author Michael Wiseman and religious leaders. https://podcasts.apple.com/us/podcast/the-bible-says-what /id1383942979

Cognitive Dissonance: Two friends, a de-converted Christian who used to be Republican and an idealistic "sometimes poet," get together to talk about news and politics. https:// dissonancepod.com.

Godless Heathens Podcast: A podcast from atheists about all sorts of topics. https://godlessheathens.podbean.com

Godless Rebelution Podcast: Founded in April 2014, *Godless Rebelution Podcast* features a former Mormon and a firefighter who served in the United States Air Force. The show pokes religion "with a sharp stick." www.godlessrebelution.com

The Radical Secular: *The Radical Secular*, by Christophe Difo and Sean Prophet, has weekly discussions of religion and politics from a liberal, cosmopolitan perspective. https://podcasts .apple.com/us/podcast/the-radical-secular/id1526238241

The Right to Reason: *The Right to Reason* is a podcast that interviews guests and discusses philosophy, politics, religion, and science. The host seeks to "generate polite and introspective discourse and fellowship in the marketplace of ideas." www.therighttoreason.com

The Scathing Atheist: *The Scathing Atheist* is a weekly look at religion and church-state encroachment from the perspective of nonbelievers. https://audioboom.com/channel/scathing-atheist

The Skeptics' Guide to the Universe: A weekly science podcast known for debunking pseudoscience and promoting critical thinking. www.theskepticsguide.org

Skeptics with a K: A podcast about science and reason brought to you by the Merseyside Skeptics Society, based in the UK. www.merseysideskeptics.org.uk/category/podcast/skeptics -with-a-k/

The Thinking Atheist: *The Thinking Atheist* is a podcast dedicated to atheist content and community, focusing on encouraging its listeners to pursue "a personal relationship with reality." The host of the podcast is Seth Andrews, an author, a former Christian of thirty years, and a former religious broadcaster. www.thethinkingatheist.com

Social Networks and Dating Sites

Agnostic.com: A social network and dating site designed specifically for atheists, agnostics, and skeptics. https://agnostic.com

Atheist Dating Service: Atheist Dating Service is the fastest-growing cooperative of online dating sites in the world. www.atheistdatingservice.com

Atheist Passions: You have a better chance of finding Waldo on this site than you do of finding God! Atheist Passions is a free online dating and social networking site specifically for freethinking singles, either atheist or agnostic. www.atheistpassions.com

Atheist Zone: A community-based social network focused on bringing freethinkers together and breaking misconceptions about atheism. https://atheistzone.com

Elite Singles: Elite Singles has atheist-specific dating services and also caters to other mature and intelligent singles with broader interests. www.elitesingles.com/atheist-dating

FreeThinker Match: A dating website for freethinkers with more than fifteen thousand members. www.freethinkermatch.com

The Secular Web: The Secular Web is an online community of nonbelievers dedicated to the pursuit of knowledge, understanding and tolerance. www.infidels.org

Religious Literacy

Religion Communicators Council: The Religion Communicators Council promotes religious literacy and helps people talk about the topic of religion. https://religioncommunicators.org/religious-literacy/

Religion in the Curriculum: The Anti-Defamation League, which seeks to "stop the defamation of the Jewish people, and to secure justice and fair treatment to all," provides a guide for educators to teach about religion without violating the rights of their students. www.adl.org/education/resources /tools-and-strategies/religion-in-public-schools/curriculum

Religious Literacy Project: Harvard Divinity School's Religious Literacy Project hopes to clarify misunderstandings about religion and provide a basic understanding of the world faiths that shape our society, from an academic perspective. https://rlp.hds.harvard.edu

The Skeptic's Annotated Bible: *The Skeptic's Annotated Bible* includes the entire text of the King James Version of the Bible in which violent, unbelievable, and contradictory passages are highlighted, and the parts of the Bible that are never read in any church, Bible study group, or Sunday school class are emphasized. www.skepticsannotatedbible.com

Teaching About Religion: Teaching About Religion provides academic information and teaching materials related to teaching about religion in public schools in support of an educational commitment to pluralism, acknowledgment that public schools are for students of all worldviews, and the professional understanding that public school teachers need to exercise a scrupulous neutrality regarding religion. www.teachingaboutreligion.com

Teaching Tolerance: Teaching Tolerance provides a lesson for anyone to explore the world's various religious traditions and learn how to create an ongoing respectful dialogue about tolerance. www.tolerance.org/classroom-resources/tolerance-lessons/taking-a-closer-look-at-religions-around-the-world

Book Recommendations

The God Delusion by Richard Dawkins

God Is Not Great: How Religion Poisons Everything by Christopher Hitchens

Outgrowing God: A Beginner's Guide by Richard Dawkins

Letter to a Christian Nation by Sam Harris

Mistakes Were Made (but Not by Me) by Carol Tavris and Elliot Aronson

The Demon-Haunted World: Science as a Candle in the Dark by Carl Sagan

The Righteous Mind: Why Good People Are Divided by Politics and Religion by Jonathan Haidt

Emancipation of a Black Atheist by D. K. Evans

Confessions of a Former Fox News Christian by Seth Andrews

RESOURCES AND SUPPORT

A Manual for Creating Atheists by Peter Boghossian

God: The Failed Hypothesis: How Science Shows That God Does Not Exist by Victor J. Stenger

50 Simple Questions for Every Christian by Guy P. Harrison

Religious Literacy: What Every American Needs to Know—And Doesn't by Stephen Prothero

The Believing Brain by Michael Shermer

How We Know What Isn't So by Thomas Gilovich

Unreasonable Faith: How William Lane Craig Overstates the Case for Christianity by James Fodor

God's Gravediggers: Why No Deity Exists by Raymond Bradley

The Falling Star by Jon Hammond

The Case Against Miracles edited by John W. Loftus

How to Be Reasonable: By Someone Who Tried Everything Else by Rebecca Fox

Better Than a Turkish Prison: What I Learned From Life in a Religious Cult by Sinasta J. Colucci

Women Beyond Belief: Discovering Life without Religion edited by Karen L. Garst

Disproving Christianity and Other Secular Writings by David G. McAfee

No Sacred Cows: Investigating Myths, Cults, and the Supernatural by David G. McAfee

The Magic of Reality: How We Know What's Really True by Richard Dawkins

Why I Am Not a Christian by Bertrand Russell

Secular Parenting in a Religious World: A Practical Guide for Free-thinking Parents by Be-Asia D McKerracher

Black Freethinkers: A History of African American Secularism (Critical Insurgencies) by Christopher Cameron

INDEX